ERNEST HEMINGWAY

Peter L. Hays

A Frederick Ungar Book
CONTINUUM • NEW YORK

1990

The Continuum Publishing Company
370 Lexington Avenue
New York, NY 10017

Printed in the United States of America

Library of Congress Cataloging-in-Publication Data

Hays, Peter L., 1938–
    Ernest Hemingway / Peter L. Hays.
        p.   cm. — (Literature and life series)
    "A Frederick Ungar book."
    Includes bibliographical references.
    ISBN 0-8264-0467-7
    1. Hemingway, Ernest, 1899–1961. 2. Authors, American—20th
century—Biography. I. Title. II. Series.
PS3515.E37Z6145   1990
813'.52—dc20
    [B]   89-48556
                                                                CIP

Contents

Acknowledgments

This book could not have been written without the prior research, biographical and critical, of many Hemingway scholars. I am particularly indebted to Carlos Baker's biography, *Ernest Hemingway: A Life Story,* and to the scholarship of Philip Young, Jackson Benson, and especially Michael Reynolds, and to my friends and colleagues of the Hemingway Society.

I am also grateful to Alfred Bendixen, without whom this book would not have been written, to my children, whose expenses made it necessary, and to my loving wife, Myrna, who made the process bearable, as she makes my life delightful.

Chronology

1899   Ernest Miller Hemingway, born on July 21, Oak Park, Il-
       linois. His father a general practitioner, his mother a music
       teacher; the family vacationed each summer at a residence
       they owned at Walloon Lake in northern Michigan.

1917   Graduated from Oak Park High School and got a job on
       the Kansas City *Star*.

1918   Quit the *Star* in April to volunteer as a Red Cross ambu-
       lance driver. On July 8 he was wounded by the explosion
       of a trench mortar shell. He recuperated in Milan, where
       he met and fell in love with Agnes von Kurowsky, an
       American Red Cross nurse seven years his senior.

1919   Sailed home in January; Agnes sent a letter breaking off
       their relationship in March. Writing short stories for slick
       magazines without success.

1920   In January got a job as a companion to a young man in
       Toronto and in February as feature writer for the Toronto
       Star Weekly. Left in May for a summer at home and in
       Michigan, moved to Chicago in the fall, became a writer
       for the journal *The Cooperative Commonwealth*. Met
       Hadley Richardson; also met and befriended by short-
       story writer and novelist Sherwood Anderson.

1921   Hemingway and Hadley Richardson were married in Sep-
       tember, lived briefly in Chicago, and sailed for Paris in
       December.

1922   Practiced writing spare, unadorned descriptive sentences,
       compressed with meaning. They lived on Hadley's inherit-
       ance and feature stories that Hemingway sold to the Tor-
       onto *Star;* he made friends with and learned from the

writers Gertrude Stein, Ezra Pound, Ford Madox Ford, and James Joyce. His poems and stories began appearing in little magazines. Engaged in journalism, covering an economic conference in Genoa, the Greco-Turkish War (where he suffered from malaria), and the Lausanne Peace Conference, which settled Greece and Turkey's territorial disputes.

1923   Visited Spain that summer and saw his first bullfights. First book, *Three Stories and Ten Poems* published. He and Hadley returned to Toronto for the birth of their only child, John Hadley Nicanor, nicknamed Bumby, born October 10. At the end of the year Hemingway's second slim book, *in our time,* a collection of brief prose sketches was also printed in Paris in a very limited edition (170 copies).

1924   Returned to Paris in January, Hemingway worked on Ford Madox Ford's *transatlantic review* while writing short stories that would appear in *In Our Time.*

1925   Met Pauline Pfeiffer, who worked for Paris *Vogue,* and F. Scott Fitzgerald, author of *The Great Gatsby.* Returned to Spain and gathered materials for his first novel, begun that summer. Boni and Liveright published *In Our Time* in October. Hemingway began *Torrents of Spring,* a book that separated him from Anderson and from Liveright.

1926   *The Torrents of Spring* was published in the spring to generally good reviews, *The Sun Also Rises* published in October and did well for a first novel. He and Hadley separated.

1927   Prepared his next collection of short stories, *Men Without Women,* and married Pauline in May.

1928   Started *Farewell to Arms.* He and a pregnant Pauline sailed to America in April. Hemingway's second son, Patrick, was born in Kansas City on June 28. They moved to Key West in November, renting a house. Later that month his father committed suicide.

1929   The family sailed to Paris in April where Ernest read proof on the magazine serialization of *A Farewell to Arms.* Summered in Spain, catching up on bullfights. *Farewell* in book form was published in September, soon selling nearly eighty thousand copies.

1930 Returned to Key West and began book on bullfighting that would become *Death in the Afternoon;* worked on it while spending the summer and fall in Wyoming, fishing and hunting. A car accident in November resulted in a badly fractured upper right arm and a hospital stay of seven weeks. Broadway and Hollywood purchased rights to dramatize *Farewell.*

1931 The winter and early spring were spent recuperating. Pauline was again pregnant, and her Uncle Gus bought them a house in Key West. Sailed to Europe that spring, attended bullfights, nearly completing *Death in the Afternoon,* returned for the birth of Gregory, their second son.

1932 Revised *Death,* which was published in September to poor reviews and wrote several new short stories.

1933 Wrote and published in magazines several short stories and began the stories that would become *To Have and Have Not;* began an association with *Esquire* magazine with a fishing article, his first journalism in ten years. His third collection of short stories, *Winner Take Nothing,* was published in the fall to generally unfavorable reviews. In November set sail for a shooting safari in Africa.

1934 Stricken with amoebic dysentery and flown to Nairobi. Tension and rivalry on hunt duly reported in Hemingway's fictional account of the safari, *The Green Hills of Africa.*

1935 *Green Hills* serialized in *Scribner's Magazine.* Hemingway wrote an article for the *New Masses* accusing the government of not protecting its own veterans and workers drowned during a hurricane. *Green Hills* was published in October to mixed reviews.

1936 The Spanish Civil War began. Worked on *To Have and Have Not,* contributed money to buy ambulances for the Loyalists in the Spanish War, and in December met Martha Gellhorn, a tourist to Key West and a novelist, journalist, and social documentarian, eight years his junior.

1937 Agreed to report on the Spanish Civil War and to help with a documentary film on the subject. Martha arrived in Spain as correspondent for *Collier's.* In June he addressed the Writers' Congress in NY, then did the sound track for *The Spanish Earth* later that month, showing it at the White House. Then went to Hollywood for more fund-raising to buy ambulances and medical supplies for the Loyalists. *To Have* was published in October, again to mixed reviews. That fall he wrote his only full-length play, *The Fifth Column.*

1938 Wrote anti-Fascist articles for the leftist magazine *Ken* and short stories about the Spanish war. Sent Scribner's the mss. for *The Fifth Column and the First Forty-Nine Stories.* His first Spanish War stories began appearing in *Esquire.*

1939 Worked on *For Whom the Bell Tolls.* Martha found a place for them in Cuba, near Havana. Ernest moved in, still married to Pauline. In Wyoming that September he heard on the radio about the outbreak of World War II in Europe. Martha left in November to cover the war in Finland for *Collier's.* His second marriage ended.

1940 *The Fifth Column* opened on Broadway and Hemingway worked on completing *Bell,* published in October. He and Martha were married in Cheyenne in November after four years together. Scott Fitzgerald died of a heart attack at year's end.

1941 Martha covered the Eastern war between Japan and China for *Collier's* and Ernest accompanied her; they shared an interview with Chiang Kai-shek. The Pulitzer Prize Committee voted to give *For Whom the Bell Tolls* its prize, but the president of Columbia University vetoed it, and no prize for literature was given that year. Ernest did no major writing that year, which concluded with the attack on Pearl Harbor and America's entry into the war.

1942 Began editing a collection of classic war stories, including three of his own, created a loosely organized intelligence unit in Havana to supply the US Embassy, through him, with any information as to Nazi activities in Cuba; he also outfitted his fishing boat as a Q-boat to attract and attack German submarines.

1943 Martha left for England to cover the war for *Collier's.*

1944   Martha returned in March, having arranged for Ernest to act as a *Collier's* correspondent with the British Royal Air Force. In London Hemingway met Mary Welsh, who would become wife number four. On May 25 Hemingway was injured in an auto accident, but left the hospital on the 29th and was on a troop transport for D day, observing the invasion. Back in London his affair with Mary Welsh intensified; he flew on several RAF missions, and reached France early in July. Attached himself to the 22nd Regiment, 4th Infantry and accompanied them across Normandy. At Rambouillet, he associated himself with some Free French fighters, and on August 24 they reached the outskirts of Paris.

He rejoined the 22nd Regiment in Belgium in early September, and crossed into Germany September 12. In October he was tried for carrying arms at Rambouillet, which correspondents may not do, perjured himself, and was excused. His eldest son, Jack (Bumby) had joined the OSS, parachuted into France, been wounded and captured by German forces. Ernest rejoined the 22nd inside Germany in November for bitter fighting.

1945   He and Martha divorce.

1946   Began writing *Garden of Eden* and married Mary in March. In Wyoming in mid-July, Mary suffered a ruptured fallopian tube from an ectopic pregnancy, and Ernest saved her life.

1947   Work continued on *Garden*. Hemingway received the Bronze Star for meritorious service as a war correspondent.

1948   Critic Malcolm Cowley visited Ernest in Cuba for a biographical piece for *Life* magazine, as did Aaron Hotchner for *Cosmopolitan*. In Italy he met Adriana Ivancich, his model for Renata and his inspiration for *Across the River and into the Trees*. He wrote Charles Scribner that he was at work on a novel about the land, sea, and air.

1949   Cowley's *Life* article appeared. In Italy Ernest contracted erysipelas. Worked on *Across the River*. In New York mid-November Lillian Ross interviewed him for a *New Yorker* profile; he finished the first draft of *Across the River* in Paris.

1950   Revised the ms. in Italy; *Across the River* began to appear in *Cosmopolitan* in serial form. His behavior showed wide swings of mood, always part of his character, but more pronounced now. Lillian Ross's *New Yorker* profile was published in May. *Across the River and into the Trees* was published in September to disastrous reviews, and in December he began a draft of what was later published posthumously as *Islands in the Stream* (part of his sea novel).

1951   Began *The Old Man and the Sea* in January, finishing the draft in February. In March returned to *Islands*. His mother died June 28; Pauline died October 1 of a tumor of the adrenal medulla at the age of fifty-six.

1952   Charles Scribner died February 11; *Life* magazine published *The Old Man and the Sea* in a single issue, selling over five million copies in two days, and the hardback did very well also, to excellent reviews, refurbishing his tarnished reputation after *Across the River;* Hemingway also agreed to a film version of *The Old Man and the Sea.*

1953   In April *The Old Man and the Sea* won the 1952 Pulitzer Prize for literature. Hemingway visited Europe and then went to Africa for another safari. Hunted through the fall and early winter in southern Kenya.

1954   Took an aerial tour of southern Kenya and Uganda, and on January 23 their plane crashed; injuries were minor. They were rescued the next day, and their next plane also crashed. Hemingway suffered very serious injuries. During the summer's recuperation he began a fictionalized diary of the African events. In October, Hemingway received the Nobel Prize for literature.

1955   Continued slow progress on the African diaries. Worked on the film version of *The Old Man and the Sea,* but ended year with nephritis and hepatitis as aftermaths of plane crash.

1956   No significant writing done.

1957   He began the series of Paris sketches that would be published posthumously as *A Moveable Feast* (the misspelling is Hemingway's).

1958   Continued work on *A Moveable Feast* and also reworked *Garden of Eden.*

1959   In January, Castro overthrew Batista in Cuba; Ernest
        bought a house in Ketchum, Idaho. Went to Spain to re-
        port on rivalry between two leading matadors for *Life*
        magazine; celebrated his sixtieth birthday. Again, dis-
        played wild mood swings. Began the *Life* article in Octo-
        ber but could not control its length: magazine article
        swelled enormously.

1960   By May, his bullfighting article for *Life*, "The Dangerous
        Summer" contracted at 10,000 words, had swollen to
        120,000. Asked Hotchner for help in cutting it, which
        Hotchner did, but it was still long for *Life*, coming out in
        three consecutive issues in September. Mary checked him
        into the Mayo Clinic for physical and psychiatric care, in-
        cluding electroshock therapy for his depression.

1961   Discharged January 23 from the clinic. Back in Idaho he
        worked on arranging the order of the sketches in *A Move-
        able Feast*. In February, asked to contribute a few lines for
        a presentation volume to newly inaugurated President
        Kennedy, he could not. The writing would not come.
        Mary interrupted a suicide attempt in April, and he tried
        again twice more before he could be taken back to the
        Mayo Clinic. More electroshock therapy affected his
        short-term memory. Nevertheless, he convinced his doc-
        tors that he was well, and they discharged him on June 26
        for the long drive back to Ketchum. On Sunday morning,
        July 2, he committed suicide.

1964   Mary, with some emendations of her own, saw to the pub-
        lication of *A Moveable Feast* by Scribner's.

1970   Scribner's publishes *Islands in the Stream*.

1972   *The Nick Adams Stories* are published by Scribner's, ar-
        ranged by critic Philip Young; the volume contains sto-
        ries, previously published and unpublished, featuring Nick
        Adams.

1981   *The Selected Letters* are published, edited by Carlos Baker.

1985   A new version of *The Dangerous Summer* is issued by
        Scribner's, with an introduction by James Michener; it
        contains some material left out of the *Life* magazine ver-
        sion, but still omits much of it.

1986 Scribner's publishes *The Garden of Eden,* edited drastically from the ms. by Tom Jenks. Mary Welsh Hemingway died November 26, at the age of seventy-eight.

1987 Scribner's releases *The Complete Short Stories of Ernest Hemingway,* the Finca Vigía edition; it does not contain all Hemingway's stories, and part of what it prints are fragments of novels.

1

A Crowded Life

Ernest Miller Hemingway, named for his maternal grandfather and great uncle, was born on July 21 in his maternal grandfather's house in Oak Park (a staid suburb of Chicago), Illinois. He was the second child, the first boy among six children (the next son, Leicester, would not be born until Ernest was fifteen). His father was a general practitioner, with a large obstetric practice, who supplemented his family practice by working as a physician for Chicago insurance firms. Ernest's mother was a trained opera singer, whose congenitally weak eyes could not stand bright lights. She returned from New York to Chicago to marry the boy across the street, Clarence Edmonds Hemingway (called Ed), and become a singing teacher, much later a painter. She was strong-willed and an early feminist, whose frequent mention in the local newspaper was as Grace Hall Hemingway; she insisted on maintaining her family name, as few women then did. Doctor Hemingway neither smoked nor drank, and he and his wife were devout, pietistic Christians, raising their children in the Congregational Church. Because of her own involvement in the arts, Mrs. Hemingway allowed (and even insisted) on dance lessons for the children, in spite of her husband's protests. She hated housework, and because her voice lessons brought in more income than the doctor's wages, they hired domestic help, though Ed enjoyed cooking, baking, and canning food, and prepared many of the family's meals. The family vacationed each summer at a residence they owned at Walloon Lake in northern Michigan (where Mrs. Hemingway did cook). As a child, both in Michigan and in

Illinois, Ernest accompanied his father fishing or on nature
hikes, learning about the out-of-doors, and becoming an
avid sportsman.

At two, Ernest would insist that he was *"fraid a nothing,"* and at five he invented a tale for his grandfather
about stopping a runaway horse. Like other children, he involved himself in make-believe acts of bravado, and when
he grew up, tried to live them. From his mother he inherited
a love of music, an artistic temperament, an equally strong
will, and defective eyes, particularly the left one; from his
father he got a knowledge and love of nature, hunting, and
fishing, and he seems also to have inherited a manic-
depressive mental disorder that affected both men throughout their lives, ultimately driving both to suicide.[1]

His youth was, to all intents, normal, even idyllic on the
surface, with regular summer trips to Michigan. In June
1917 he graduated from Oak Park High School with a
good background in English literature and competence in
history, biology, arithmetic, Latin, and music. He played
cello in the school orchestra, boxed with friends, was on
the swim team and water-basketball squad, a clumsy sub-
stitute tackle in football, and also active in the high
school's literary magazine and newspaper.

Although America had entered World War I, his parents'
wishes and his own poor vision kept Ernest out of the army.
After the summer vacation of 1917, he got a job on the
Kansas City Star, then one of America's best newspapers,
living at first with one of his uncles. He covered the police
and hospital beat, an introduction to a seamier life than the
middle-class existence he had known in Oak Park. Also important for his development as a writer, the *Star* had a style
sheet that insisted that its reporters use "short sentences.
Use short first paragraphs. Use vigorous English. . . ."
These lessons reinforced the style of writing he had already
begun in high school, a plain style that would change the
face of American literature, which still favored the ornate
prose and balanced clause construction of the late nineteenth century.

At the end of six months in Kansas City he volunteered for duty as a Red Cross ambulance driver in Europe, marched before President Woodrow Wilson in New York, and sailed to Paris. He was assigned to Italy, and his first duty in Milan was carrying dead victims of a munitions plant explosion; many were women, decaying in the June heat. It was an unromantic introduction to war. His next assignment was to Schio, in the Dolomite Alps east of Milan, driving ambulances, but there was little fighting there, not enough for a romantic young man at his first war. Hemingway volunteered for Italy's eastern front as a canteen worker, someone who passed out Red Cross chocolates and cigarettes to the troops. At Fossalta di Piave, around midnight on the evening of July 8, 1918, he crawled in front of the Italian lines to a forward listening post on the banks of the Piave River; there he was hit by an exploding trench mortar shell, a missile about the size of a five-gallon can filled with scrap metal. Some 227 metal fragments and two machine-gun bullets were taken from his legs at the time (others were revealed still in place in 1950 X rays). The machine-gun bullets are problematical. They might have been in the shrapnel of the exploding shell, but the story Hemingway told others was that after recovering consciousness, despite his own wounds, he tried to carry a surviving Italian on his shoulder back to the aid station, and was hit twice by machine-gun fire; at least as likely is the possibility that he was shot again while being carried on a stretcher by others. He was the first American to be wounded in Italy and survive, and American newspapers made a hero of him (he also received two medals from Italy).

From July through October he recuperated at the Ospedale Croce Rossa in Milan, where he met and fell in love with Agnes von Kurowsky, an American Red Cross nurse seven and a half years his senior. A brief attempt to return to the battle, though he was still limping, was cut short by jaundice, and the war ended in November; his actual service at the front, thus, was just over five weeks. He left Italy in January 1919 without Agnes, believing she would

follow him to the States once he had a job enabling them to
marry, but she fell in love with an Italian officer and wrote
Hemingway of that fact in March. The news was devastat-
ing, and he took to bed for several days with a fever, seemingly more devastated psychologically by this wound than
by his physical one of the preceding summer. He suffered
from insomnia and insisted on going to sleep with the lights
on in his room.

He was still limping, still taking things easily, but also
trying to write commercial, formula stories for slick magazines like the *Saturday Evening Post,* stories that were not
bought.[2] He stayed in Michigan long after the family left
Walloon Lake, writing through the fall, and meeting a
woman from Toronto who hired him as a companion for
her lame son. In Toronto, Hemingway also got a position
writing feature stories for the *Toronto Star Weekly,* beginning in February 1920, but he quit in the summer to return
to Upper Michigan. At Walloon Lake that summer an argument with his parents caused a family split, so he moved to
Chicago in the fall and pieced out a living with part-time
jobs until he became a writer for *The Cooperative Com-
monwealth,* a monthly magazine of the Cooperative Society
of America. That fall he met Hadley Richardson, a St.
Louis woman, eight years his senior; he also met and was
befriended by short-story writer and novelist Sherwood
Anderson. The impression he gave others was of an in-
tensely vital young man, very shy, who overcame his shy-
ness with spurts of brusque defensiveness.

Hemingway and Hadley Richardson were married in
September, lived briefly in Chicago, and sailed for Paris in
December with letters of introduction from Sherwood
Anderson to modernist experimenter Gertrude Stein, and
found a flat in a working-class district of Paris on rue de
Cardinal Lemoine. There, with Hadley's and Anderson's
encouragement, Ernest abandoned his attempt at slick commercial fiction and practiced writing spare, unadorned, descriptive sentences, compressed with meaning, "one true
sentence," as he put it.[3] They lived on Hadley's inheritance
and feature stories that Hemingway continued to sell to the

Toronto Star Daily and the *Star Weekly;* he made friends
with and learned from such modernists as Gertrude Stein,
the poet Ezra Pound, and novelists Ford Madox Ford and
James Joyce. Hemingway's poems and stories began appearing in little magazines, the New Orleans *Double Dealer* and
Poetry; for the *Star* he covered an international economic
conference in Genoa, the Greco-Turkish War (where he suffered from lice and malaria), and the Lausanne Peace Conference, which settled Greece and Turkey's territorial
disputes. He also sent Greco-Turkish War dispatches to the
International News Service (unscrupulously selling both
agencies the same stories). He wired Hadley in Paris to join
him for a skiing vacation after the Lausanne conference,
and she brought his stories and poems so that he could
work on them. The valise containing all his writing, except
for two stories that were elsewhere, was stolen from her
train compartment. He had to begin over.

In the summer of 1923 Hemingway visited Spain and saw
his first bullfights in June, and returned to Spain from Paris
in July for the Pamplona festival. A Paris acquaintance who
planned a series of modernist works—verse by William
Carlos Williams and Mina Loy, stories by Hemingway—
accepted, in fact, both stories and poems from Hemingway
and published them as Hemingway's first book that summer, *Three Stories and Ten Poems* (1923). Then he and
Hadley returned to Toronto for the birth of their first child,
John Hadley Nicanor (the last name, for a bullfighter they
admired, Nicanor Villalta, but the baby was nicknamed
Bumby), born October 10, while Hemingway was returning
from a news assignment in New York City for the *Daily
Star.* By the end of the year Hemingway's second book, *in
our time,* a collection of brief prose sketches, was printed in
Paris by another friend in a very limited edition (170 cop-
ies, publication date given is 1924).

The Hemingways returned to Paris in January 1924 to
a flat over a sawmill on Notre Dame des Champs, near
the Luxembourg Gardens; Ernest acted as (unpaid) assistant
editor to Ford Madox Ford's *transatlantic review* while
writing short stories that would appear in *In Our*

Time, separated by the sketches already published in *in our time* as interchapters. The titles, being largely the same, are confusing: *in our time* is a limited edition of one-or-two-paragraph-long vignettes; *In Our Time,* with capital letters, is Hemingway's first American book, a collection of short stories with the shorter vignettes appearing as interchapters.

The summer was spent in Spain, at bullfights. The damp Paris winter was avoided by a skiing trip to Austria, where Hemingway learned that the American publishing firm of Boni & Liveright, Sherwood Anderson's publisher, had accepted *In Our Time.* When the Hemingways returned to Paris, they met Pauline Pfeiffer, who worked on Paris *Vogue* and who was four years older than Ernest. That spring Hemingway also met F. Scott Fitzgerald, author of *The Great Gatsby,* and for years a close friend.

Realizing that he needed a novel to solidify his reputation, that summer in Spain at the Pamplona festival Ernest assimilated the materials for his first, *The Sun Also Rises,* a roman à clef based on his friends and experiences that summer, but fictionally altered.

In Our Time was published in October 1925, and when reviews compared him to Sherwood Anderson, Hemingway wrote a parody of Anderson's stylistic excesses in *The Torrents of Spring.* *Torrents* (published 1926) was Ernest's declaration of independence, from Anderson, who had been his friend and mentor, and from Liveright, to whom he had to submit his next book after *In Our Time.* They did reject *Torrents,* Anderson being their leading writer, and Hemingway was now free to sign a contract with Scribner's, not only an older, more prestigious firm, but also one with a magazine of its own in which Hemingway could publish his short stories.

The Hemingways wintered again in Schruns, Austria, joined by Pauline Pfeiffer. In February 1926 Hemingway returned to New York, disengaged himself from Liveright, and signed a contract with Scribner's for *Torrents* and the unfinished *The Sun Also Rises.* On his return to Europe, Hemingway spent time with Pauline in Paris before returning to Hadley in Schruns; there, he finished revising *The Sun Also Rises*, his novel of life among expatriates in Paris and Spain. The Hemingways spent the summer on the Riviera with Scott and Zelda Fitzgerald, among others, and "return[ed] to Paris to set up separate residences" (the clause that concludes Hemingway's "A Canary for One," a fictional version of their train trip). Scribner's published *The Sun Also Rises* that fall, and it did well for a first novel, many critics regarding it as a satirical portrait of the dissolute life led by members of the Lost Generation amidst the wasteland of postwar Europe. Hemingway assigned the royalties to Hadley and Bumby and applied for a divorce.

Throughout the winter and spring of 1927, Hemingway prepared *Men Without Women*, his next collection of short stories, written in France, Austria, and Spain over the past several years. Scribner's practice was to follow the publication of a full-length work with a short-story collection so that each book would benefit from the publicity engendered by the other. The stories of *Men Without Women*, together with those of *In Our Time*, represent most of Hemingway's best short stories, and since one could make the case that Hemingway is a better short-story writer than novelist, one could also say that these books contain most of his best fiction. In May, he married Pauline Pfeiffer, a woman who, like Hadley, was not only older than he, but richer. Pauline's father owned large tracts of cotton land around Piggott, Arkansas, and her uncle Gus Pfeiffer had a controlling interest in Hudnut cosmetics and perfumes. Their honeymoon was spent on the Mediterranean, summer was spent in Spain, and Hemingway began a new novel that was never finished or published. *Men Without Women* was published in October and did well.

In Paris the following spring he began *A Farewell to Arms*, based in part on his experiences in World War I and with Agnes von Kurowsky, and in April he and a pregnant Pauline sailed to the US, spending some time in Key West before visiting her relatives in Arkansas and then going on to Kansas City for the birth of Hemingway's second son, Patrick, on June 28, 1928. Escaping the heat of the Midwest and his noisy son, Hemingway went fishing in Wyoming, where he finished the first draft of *A Farewell to Arms*. He and Pauline rented a house in Key West, where Ernest worked on revising *Farewell*, interrupted by the news of his father's suicide in November and the author's trip back to Oak Park.

In April 1929 the family sailed back to Paris. Hemingway read proof on the serialization of *Farewell* that *Scribner's Magazine* was bringing out. That summer he again went to Spain for the bullfights and decided to explain the art of bullfighting, which he saw as undergoing a decline, in a book that would describe the essence of bullfighting, not just as a spectator sport, but as an art form, combining balletic movements with tragedy; that book, *Death in the Afternoon*, also included his own pronouncements on art. *A Farewell to Arms* in book form was published in September to excellent reviews and initial sales, but the 1929 Crash was only a month away. In January 1930 they sailed back to the US and Key West, where Hemingway worked on the bullfighting book, *Death in the Afternoon*, continuing that work during the summer and fall in Wyoming, between fishing and hunting. In a car accident in November, Hemingway so badly fractured his upper right arm that a surgeon had to operate and sew the muscle back together, and Hemingway had to spend seven weeks in a Billings, Montana, hospital. Although the Depression had slowed sales of *Farewell*, his income benefited from the sale of dramatization rights to the novel to Broadway and Hollywood.

Pauline became pregnant again that winter and her Uncle Gus bought the Hemingways a house in Key West. They sailed to Europe in the spring, and despite the political upheavals that would lead to the Spanish Civil War, Hemingway returned to Spain for the bullfights and to work on *Death in the Afternoon*. They returned to the US in September, going to St. Louis for the birth of Gregory in November and the completion of the draft of *Death in the Afternoon*. The spring of 1932 was spent revising the manuscript and writing short stories for inclusion in a new collection. Hemingway frequently visited Cuba for morning writing, afternoon fishing, and he and Pauline spent the summer and fall in Wyoming. *Death in the Afternoon* was published in September, and most American critics, in the depth of the Depression, found it irrelevant to their social concerns; others attacked Hemingway's macho posturing.

Stories that would appear in the next collection, *Winner Take Nothing,* were published in *Scribner's Magazine* and *Cosmopolitan* in 1933. His Cuban fishing trips and the political unrest there served as background for stories that would grow into his third novel, *To Have and Have Not;* as the title indicates, critics' complaints that Hemingway was ignoring economic concerns had finally sunk in. *To Have and Have Not* concerns Harry Morgan, husband, father, fishing-boat operator, rum runner, smuggler, and killer (he is named for the Caribbean pirate of the seventeenth century), and his difficulties of maintaining family and pride during disastrous economic times. Hemingway began as association with *Esquire* magazine with a fishing story, his first piece of feature journalism in ten years. In Spain that summer he continued work on *To Have and Have Not,* and in Paris that fall he wrote to *Esquire* readers that the Parisians were resigned to a coming war. *Winner Take Nothing* was published that fall to generally unfavorable reviews, deservedly so, for the short stories, except for "A Clean, Well-Lighted Place," represent a falling off from Hemingway's sharpest, most incisive stories. In November, Ernest and Pauline set sail for East Africa and a shooting safari paid for by Uncle Gus.

A severe case of amoebic dysentery, requiring a plane flight back to Nairobi, provided Ernest with the nucleus for "Snows of Kilimanjaro," and an anecdote told by their guide provided the basis for "The Short Happy Life of Francis Macomber." A companion on the hunt consistently shot better trophy animals than Hemingway, creating much tension: Hemingway could not endure being bested in anything he committed himself to. He kept a journal of his experiences, a journal that, with fictional rearrangement and aesthetic heightening, would become *Green Hills of Africa,* his second book of nonfiction. Hemingway claims in the

book's foreword that "the writer has attempted to write an
absolutely true book to see whether the shape of a country
and the pattern of a month's action can, if truly presented,
compete with a work of the imagination." On their way
back to Key West, Hemingway purchased a thirty-eight-
foot, twin-diesel-engined boat, which he renamed the *Pilar,*
after a nickname for Pauline and after the shrine and festival of the Virgen del Pilar in Zaragoza, Spain. Pauline was
a Catholic, and Hemingway's marriage to her was in the
Catholic church; he practiced Catholicism, distinctly after
his own fashion (which is to say, irregularly), from his marriage to Pauline until the end of his life.

The first half of 1935 was spent fishing at Bimini and
Key West; *Green Hills* was serialized in *Scribner's,* then
published in book form in October, where leftist critics
continued to revile the conspicuous consumption displayed
by a safari at a time when many people were out of work
and suffering; others criticized the mentality of a talented
author wasting his time chasing and shooting animals. Another incident, however, occurred to move Hemingway
deeper into forms of political involvement. A Force 5 hurricane struck the Keys in September. Key West was only
lightly damaged, but further north heavy damage was in-
flicted: government work camps employing World War I
veterans to build the Florida East Coast Railway were completely destroyed and nearly a thousand people were
drowned (the official government count is under five hundred, but Hemingway assumed that for each body retrieved,
another was blown away to sea). Although notice of the
storm appeared in the Key West newspaper, there had been
little or no warning, no protection for veterans on Keys ris-
ing only a few feet above the sea and housed in tents. Hemingway sailed the *Pilar* to Lower Matecumbe Key
immediately after the storm to do what he could to help;
the scene reminded him of the Milan munitions factory
where, in World War I, he had had to carry away the dead.
In reaction, he wrote a brief article for the Communist
journal *The New Masses,* accusing the government of not
caring for its veterans or protecting its workers.

The Spanish Civil War began in the summer of 1936, while Hemingway was in Wyoming, hunting, fishing, and working on *To Have and Have Not*. He contributed money to buy ambulances for the Loyalist, anti-Fascist forces in Spain, and in Key West in December, he met a twenty-eight-year-old novelist, journalist, and social documentarian, Martha Gellhorn. Signing a contract to cover the Spanish War for a group of American papers, and agreeing also to participate in making a documentary film of the subject, Hemingway reached Spain in mid-March of 1937; Martha arrived at the end of the month as a correspondent for *Collier's* magazine. Much of April was spent in filming *The Spanish Earth*, for which Ernest wrote the narrative, later even recording it on the sound track, replacing actor Orson Welles. By this time, if not before, he and Martha were lovers. In June Hemingway addressed the Writers' Congress in New York, raising funds for nonmilitary aid for the Loyalist, Republican cause, and the next month he was present at a showing of *The Spanish Earth* at the White House (Eleanor Roosevelt was an admirer of Martha and her writing). Hemingway then went to Hollywood for more fund-raising. After correcting proof on *To Have and Have Not* (pieces of which had appeared in *Cosmopolitan* and *Esquire*), he sailed again for Spain. *To Have and Have Not* was published in October to largely unfavorable reviews, despite its social and economic content, which is not central to the novel. That fall, Hemingway wrote *The Fifth Column*, his only full-length play (a one-act play, "Today Is Friday," was published in *Men Without Women*); it was set in the Spanish Civil War, involved spies and secret agents, and the inner struggle between public responsibilities and personal desires.

In the winter of 1938 he rejoined Pauline in Paris and they sailed to the US together, but by April Hemingway was back in Spain, at the war, and with Martha. In May he returned to the US for fishing and writing: anti-Fascist articles for magazines and short stories about the war that would later appear in *Esquire*. By the end of summer he had sent Scribner's the introduction and manuscript for his

collected short stories, to be published together with his
play as *The Fifth Column and the First Forty-Nine Stories*.
The printed play was not received well, more criticism of
macho posturing, but Hemingway's skill as a short-story
writer received new praise. In November Hemingway made
his last visit to Spain before the collapse of the Loyalists
and the victory of Franco's Rebel troops in March of 1939.

The winter of 1938 and the spring of 1939 were spent in
Cuba on short stories and on *For Whom the Bell Tolls,* begun the previous fall. Martha found a house for them fifteen miles outside of Havana named Finca Vigía (Lookout
Farm) and refurbished it at her own expense. Hemingway
moved in, still married to Pauline. World War II began in
Europe while Hemingway was hunting and fishing in Wyoming, and working on *Bell,* his best extended writing in
over a decade; it concerned a dynamiter working with Loyalist partisans behind Rebel lines in an attempt to blow a
bridge coincident with a Loyalist attack and so prevent the
arrival of Rebel reinforcements to the scene of the attack.
As with *A Farewell to Arms,* Hemingway combines love
with war, but in both novels he attacks the savagery, brutality, and absurdity of war on both sides of the conflict.

Pauline joined him in Wyoming, but he left her in October to join Martha at Sun Valley, Idaho; Martha, in turn,
left him temporarily in November to cover the war in Finland for *Collier's.* Hemingway returned to the house in Key
West for Christmas to discover that Pauline had taken the
children to New York and that his second marriage was
over; he moved to Cuba.

The Fifth Column (the play was published separately that
year by Scribner's) opened on Broadway in March 1940,
starring Franchot Tone and Lee J. Cobb, produced by the
Theatre Guild and supported by their subscription list;
nevertheless it ran for only eighty-seven performances.
Throughout most of the year Hemingway worked on *For
Whom the Bell Tolls;* finishing his manuscript in July, then
revising it in both typescript and galleys, as was his custom.
Book-of-the-Month took it as its October selection, guaranteeing good sales, and the film rights went for the highest

price then paid for a book, $100,000 plus a percentage of the book sales. Reviews of the book were good from those critics not so indissolubly wedded to either the political right or left that they felt in some way attacked, with the additional exception of those who found Hemingway's love scenes embarrassing, and its first printing was seventy-five thousand copies.

Hemingway and Martha Gellhorn were married in Cheyenne, Wyoming, after nearly four years together, and as a Christmas present to her he purchased the Finca Vigía. The year ended with news from Scribner's of the death by heart attack of Scott Fitzgerald. Martha was given the assignment by Collier's to cover the Eastern war between China and Japan, and Hemingway accompanied her to Hong Kong, Shaokuan, and Chungking, contributing his own impressions to another magazine; they even shared an interview with General Chiang Kai-shek. On their return to America they shared their impressions with Naval Intelligence. Hemingway's For Whom the Bell Tolls was nominated unanimously by the Pulitzer Prize Committee for the 1941 prize in literature, but Nicholas Murray Butler the president of Columbia University, which bestowed the awards, vetoed the nomination. No prize for literature was given that year, for which Butler never explained his reasons, simply telling the committee to "consider before you ask the University to be associated with an award for a work of this nature."[4] Perhaps Hemingway's overt sexuality in the novel or his sympathies with left-wing Loyalists alienated very conservative President Butler.

As part of the propaganda effort of the war, Hemingway was asked by Crown Publishers to edit a collection of classic war stories, Men at War, and included three of his own (in his case, selections from Farewell and Bell, as well as a short story about the Spanish War). Hemingway also created a loosely organized intelligence unit in Havana, the "Crook Factory," to supply the American Embassy, through him, with any information as to Nazi activities in Cuba; he also outfitted the Pilar as a Q-boat to attract and attack German submarines (Hemingway's romanticism and enthusiasm exceeded his military value in these endeavors). *Men at War* appeared in October, and spy catching in Cuba was assigned by the government to the FBI.

Bumby (Jack Hemingway) left Dartmouth in 1943 for Officer Candidate School and army service, and the movie version of *Bell* was released in July with Gary Cooper and Ingrid Bergman in the lead roles. Martha completed a novel and left for England to cover the war for *Collier's*. Again, Hemingway did no significant writing that year, although *Bell* continued to sell well.

Martha returned in March, having arranged for Ernest to act as a *Collier's* correspondent with the British Royal Air Force. Martha sailed back to Europe in May on a cargo vessel carrying explosives, the only transport that she, as a civilian, could arrange; Ernest, with his greater reputation, was given a seat on a plane and flew to London that month, where he soon met Mary Welsh, who would become his fourth and last wife, though she was also married at the time. After a party, Hemingway's driver ran into a water tower in blacked-out London the morning of May 25; Hemingway suffered badly bruised knees, a concussion, and a deep wound where the rearview mirror mount entered his head. He left the hospital on May 29. Nevertheless, he was on a troop transport for D day, transferred to a landing craft and observed the invasion and the landing of troops, though he, himself, did not land that day. Martha, on the other hand, did. Later in June the German V-1 bombing of London began, and his affair with Mary Welsh intensified; he flew on several RAF missions, most intended to keep him out of trouble's way, and finally reached France early in July.

Ernest soon attached himself to the 22nd Regiment, 4th Infantry, and accompanied them across Normandy. At Rambouillet, he associated himself with some Free French fighters as liaison, translating and transmitting their information to the US Army, participating in their activities, and pretending to be a guerrilla leader comparable to Confederate raider Colonel John Mosby, or Francis Marion, the Swamp Fox of the Revolutionary War. (Hemingway was an avid reader of military history, and he had just reread a great deal for *Men at War*.) In August he had to dive from a motorcycle to avoid German fire and struck his head, his second concussion in three months. On August 24, Hemingway and his irregulars reached the outskirts of Paris. On the twenty-fifth, Hemingway, as he fondly claimed, liberated the Travellers Club and the Ritz Hotel.

He rejoined the 22nd Regiment in Belgium in early September, and crossed into Germany on the twelfth. In October he was tried by the army for carrying arms at Rambouillet, which correspondents may not do, perjured himself, and was excused (the penalty would have been loss of his correspondent's accreditation and immediate passage home). That same month he found out that Bumby, who had joined the OSS and had parachuted into France behind German lines, was missing in action; Jack Hemingway had been wounded and captured by German forces. Martha, who had been frequently separated from him over the last years, conducting her own journalistic career, and who knew of Hemingway's affair with Mary Welsh, asked for a divorce. Hemingway rejoined the 22nd inside Germany in November for the Hürtgenwald Campaign, where the regiment sustained 2,600 casualties in two weeks. He went back to Paris with a bad chest cold, then rejoined the 4th Division in late December when the Germans counterattacked in the Battle of the Bulge.

Hemingway returned to Paris in January and to Cuba in March to prepare the Finca for Mary, who arrived in May. Jack, freed from a prisoner-of-war camp, arrived to recuperate in June. At the end of that month, Ernest, with Mary, was in still another auto accident; more damage to his knees, ribs, and his third concussion in two years. Mary received her divorce in August. Hemingway wrote nothing except letters, and introductions to other people's books, but did sell the rights for two of his published stories to Hollywood. His and Martha's divorce was official December 21, 1945.

He began writing the manuscript of what has since been published posthumously as *The Garden of Eden* and mar-

ried Mary in March. They planned a vacation at Sun Valley
and set out driving there. In Wyoming in mid-July, Mary
suffered a ruptured fallopian tube from an ectopic pregnancy, and her veins collapsed in the local hospital Ernest
had taken her to. She was given up for dead. Hemingway
forced the intern to probe surgically for a vein, find one,
and introduce plasma—and Mary recovered. In early September they were at Sun Valley with Ernest's younger sons
(Jack had returned to college at the University of Montana).
Hemingway continued working on *Eden* throughout the
winter and spring, in Idaho and Cuba. Another car wreck,
this one the boys', resulted in a bad concussion for Patrick
and more nurse duty for Ernest. In June, Hemingway received the Bronze Star for his "meritorious service" as a
war correspondent. In August he was diagnosed as having
high blood pressure, as well as being badly overweight.
Late summer and fall of 1947 were spent at Sun Valley,
Idaho, still working sporadically at *Eden*.

Critic Malcolm Cowley visited Ernest in Cuba in February 1948 for a biographical piece for *Life* magazine, as did
Aaron Hotchner, who asked Hemingway for an article for
Cosmopolitan. The younger sons joined him for a summer
of fishing, and the elder Hemingways sailed for Italy in the
fall. Ernest wrote a travel piece about the Gulf Stream for
Holiday magazine, and while pheasant shooting on the
Tagliamento River (into which Lieutenant Henry had dived
in *A Farewell to Arms*) met young Adriana Ivancich, his
inspiration for the soon-to-be-written *Across the River and
into the Trees* and his model for Renata, its heroine. At the
time, however, he wrote Charles Scribner that he was at
work on an epic novel about the land, sea, and air, *Eden*
having been laid aside, unfinished.

In January 1949 Cowley's *Life* article appeared, and a
series of illnesses and accidents befell the Hemingways.
Mary broke an ankle skiing, and Ernest got an infection in
an eye, probably from gunpowder blowback while shooting, that spread and became the full-blown skin disease
erysipelas. He abandoned the long epic novel and turned his
attention to one with Venice at its center (*Across the River*),

and the Hemingways sailed for home at the end of April where Ernest continued working on *River*, an account of a fifty-year-old professional soldier and veteran of three wars who faces imminent death by heart attack in Venice in the loving company of a nineteen-year-old countess; Hemingway celebrated his fiftieth birthday in July. Hotchner arranged to have the new novel serialized in *Cosmopolitan*, prior to book publication. Ernest and Mary left Cuba for New York in mid-November, where Lillian Ross interviewed him for a *New Yorker* profile, then sailed for Paris, where Ernest finished the first draft of *Across the River*.

He revised the manuscript in Italy, where bad luck continued to plague them: Mary broke her other ankle. They sailed to New York at the end of March, where *Across the River* had begun its serialized appearance the previous month, and reached Cuba in April. Ernest worked on the galleys of *Across the River*. His behavior showed wide swings of mood, always part of his character, but more pronounced now, exhibiting the same symptoms of mental instability that his father had. Lillian Ross's *New Yorker* profile was published in May, and Hemingway, in a boating accident in July, slipped and hit his head against metal clamps: still another concussion. He wrote two children's fables about Venice for *Holiday*. *Across the River* was published in September of 1950 to disastrous reviews that criticized the slackness and self-indulgence in the prose that seemed a bad parody of the early, taut Hemingway style.

In December of that year Ernest began writing a draft of what was later published posthumously as *Islands in the Stream;* it was a part of the land, air, sea novel that he had written about to Charles Scribner. Then in January he turned his attention to *The Old Man and the Sea* (the nucleus of which had appeared in *Esquire* in 1936), and the story flowed easily and smoothly, the first draft being done by mid-February. The story of an elderly Cuban fisherman who catches a giant marlin, only to have his prize taken from him by sharks, it embodies in near-fable form Hemingway's philosophy that "a man can be destroyed but not defeated." In March he returned to his sea novel (*Islands*), expanding it with Thomas Hudson's submarine-hunting activities, based on his own wartime experiences on the *Pilar.* In March 1951 his Venetian fables appeared in *Holiday* and a hunting account in *True.* Grace Hall Hemingway died June 28, and in August Mary left to go to Minneapolis to care for her father, ill with cancer. Pauline died on October 1, and Charles Scribner, his publisher for twenty-six years, died the following February.

In April 1952, Hemingway began a short story based on an incident when he was a boy in Michigan and had shot a protected blue heron and had avoided game marshals who had come to serve him with a summons; the story, "The Last Good Country" remains unfinished but is printed in *The Nick Adams Stories* and *The Complete Short Stories of Ernest Hemingway.* The Book-of-the-Month-Club selected *Old Man and the Sea,* guaranteeing good sales, and *Life* magazine decided to print the novella in its entirety in a September issue, something *Life* had never done before. More than five million copies were sold in two days, and the hardcover editions also did very well, to excellent reviews, refurbishing the reputation that had suffered with *Across the River.* Hemingway also agreed to a film version of the book, which in April 1953 finally won Hemingway the Pulitzer Prize for Literature (for 1952), after it had been denied to *For Whom the Bell Tolls.*

In June 1953 the Hemingways sailed for Europe, for Ernest's first visit to Spain since the end of the civil war and the beginning of Franco's rule. Afterward they sailed to Africa for another safari, this time with Ernest and *Look* magazine paying the bills. They hunted through the fall and early winter in southern Kenya. As a belated Christmas present to Mary, Ernest arranged an aerial tour of southern Kenya and Uganda, and on January 23 their chartered sight-seeing plane hit a telegraph wire and crashed near Murchison Falls in Uganda; injuries were minor, including a sprained shoulder for Ernest. They were rescued the next day, taken by boat (the same boat used in filming *The African Queen*) to Butiaba, Uganda, where a plane would take them to Entebbe. On takeoff, it too crashed. This time

Hemingway suffered a collapsed lower intestine, ruptured liver, kidney, and spleen, a crushed vertebra, a very severe concussion (possibly a skull fracture), deafness in one ear, and burns on his head, face, and arms, which were compounded the next month when he tried to help put out a brush fire and fell into it. The Hemingways sailed north, through the Suez Canal, reaching Venice in late March, for more medical treatment and rest and recuperation. Although the pain and discomfort had been severe, Hemingway enjoyed reading the flattering obituary notices that were published when news of his crashes became news of his death. Because of his back injury, he frequently typed standing up thereafter.

Joined by Aaron Hotchner, later the author of the worshipful but inaccurate *Papa Hemingway* (1966), Ernest was driven to Madrid in May for the bullfights, where Mary had gone ahead. The Hemingways sailed home to Cuba in June. During the summer's continued recuperation Ernest at first wrote only letters, then began a fictionalized diary of the African events, among his papers at the John F. Kennedy Library in Boston, but not yet published. In October 1954, Hemingway received the Nobel Prize for literature.

He continued slow progress on the African diaries through the winter and into 1955. In August a film crew arrived for the filming of *The Old Man and the Sea,* and Hemingway's back was well enough to do some fishing for them, but they were unsuccessful in catching a very large fish for the cameras, and the largely unproductive year ended with bouts of nephritis and hepatitis, results of his damaged kidney and liver.

In April and May of 1956 he and Mary were in Peru with the film crew, trying to catch a giant marlin; Ernest did catch one weighing 680 pounds. An article for *Look* magazine was his only published writing that year, but he did write one story later sold to *The Atlantic* and four stories based on World War II experiences. The Hemingways sailed for Europe, stayed briefly in Paris, and drove to Spain in September for the final bullfights of the season.

Ernest's blood pressure and cholesterol were very high, and he was put on a fat-free, low alcohol diet, and forbidden by his doctor to engage in sexual activities. The year ended in Paris at the Ritz Hotel, where two trunks belonging to Ernest had been found, stored since 1928, containing notebooks of his writing and clothes (or so, at least, Hemingway claimed; one researcher doubts it).[5]

The Hemingways sailed back to Cuba in January 1957, Ernest under medical care for blood pressure and cholesterol. He wrote another poor story for *The Atlantic* ("A Man of the World") and participated in the efforts to free Ezra Pound from St. Elizabeth's Hospital in Washington, where Pound had been incarcerated as insane following a trial for treason after the war. He began the series of Paris reminiscences that would be published posthumously as *A Moveable Feast* (the misspelling is Hemingway's). At the same time, he also reworked *Garden of Eden,* and his health—weight, blood pressure, cholesterol, liver—seemed better.

In January 1959, Fidel Castro's revolution was successful in Cuba. Ernest bought a furnished house in Ketchum on seventeen acres of land near where he had long hunted and fished. By May he and Mary were in Spain, where Hemingway was going to cover a bullfighting rivalry between Spain's two leading matadors as an article for *Life* magazine, and where he celebrated his sixtieth birthday. Again, he displayed erratic mood swings. Using his notes from the summer he began the *Life* article in October, and what was to have been merely an article swelled uncontrollably. Later that month they sailed for New York and Ernest submitted his typescript of *A Moveable Feast* to Scribner's.

By the following May, his bullfighting article for *Life,* contracted at 10,000 words, had swollen to 120,000. Ernest complained of confusion, a sad premonition, especially in conjunction with his mood swings, echoing his father's syndrome. He urged Aaron Hotchner to join him in Cuba to cut the bullfighting manuscript, "The Dangerous Summer," which Hotchner did, but it was still too long for publication by *Life* as one article. He quietly celebrated his sixty-first birthday, his last, in New York, before flying to Spain to check final details for "The Dangerous Summer." His hosts found him severely depressed, lonely, afraid, suffering ennui, insomnia, loss of memory, and delusions of persecution. "The Dangerous Summer" came out in three consecutive *Life* issues in September. (Scribner's has since published a reedited version, posthumously.) Ernest flew to Mary in New York City in October. She got him on the train to Idaho. Among his delusions of persecution was the belief that the FBI was following him. But this was not a delusion: they were and had been since he had raised money for the Spanish Loyalists in 1936. Again his blood pressure was dangerously high, even though his weight was down to 175 from over 200 pounds. On November 30, 1960, Ernest was entered into the Mayo Clinic for physical and psychiatric care. A mild case of diabetes was also found, in addition to the blood, liver, and kidney problems, and hemochromatosis (a rare blood disease) was also suspected. To treat his depression, electroshock therapy was begun.

Hemingway was discharged January 23, 1961, from the clinic. Back in Idaho he worked on arranging the order of the sketches in *A Moveable Feast*. In February, asked to contribute a few lines for a presentation volume to newly inaugurated President Kennedy, he could not. The writing would not come. Mary interrupted a suicide attempt in April, and before Ernest could be taken back to the Mayo Clinic he tried again. En route, at a fuel stop, he tried again by attempting to walk into the propellers of a taxiing plane. At the clinic, there was more shock therapy, which destroyed his short-term memory. Nevertheless, Ernest convinced his doctors that he was well, and they discharged him on June 26 for the long drive back to Ketchum. On Sunday morning, July 2, 1961, he put two shells in a shotgun, pressed the shotgun against his forehead, and committed suicide,[6] a week before the anniversary of his wounding in Italy, forty-four years before, and three weeks before his sixty-second birthday, freed from bodily pain and the inability to write, but with his position in literature secure.

2

≈≈≈≈≈≈≈≈≈≈≈≈≈≈≈≈≈≈≈≈≈≈≈≈≈≈≈≈≈≈≈≈≈≈

Creation of a New Prose

In the period immediately before World War I, there was a revolution in art of all forms. The Impressionists in France, late in the nineteenth century, had abandoned photographic realism to imply their emotional impressions of a scene, and by the time of Picasso and Braque at the end of the first decade of the twentieth century, painters were analyzing shapes, deconstructing them for component elements; or, in the case of abstract expressionism later, doing away with representational reality altogether. Sculpture, similarly, abandoned accurate representation, from the mechanical constructions of Marcel Duchamp to the abstracted stylizations of Constantin Brancusi. Arnold Schoenberg, the composer, used a twelve-tone scale rather than the conventional octave, and with composers like Igor Stravinski and Charles Ives introduced atonal, dissonant passages into music, because—among other reasons—the world their music reflected was not always harmonious and sweet, and also because they did not want to create in the same manner as their predecessors had; they wanted to extend the range of their art. Beyond the arts, Sigmund Freud demonstrated that surface reality was misleading and that what was unseen could be equally important; and in physics, Werner Heisenberg postulated that complete and accurate depictions of phenomena were impossible.

In writing, similar forms of revolution were going on. James Joyce was insisting on removing the obvious presence of the author and his editorial comments, either overtly with such intrusions as a Henry Fielding or William Thackeray might make—"Dear and gentle reader, let us now consider whether this act was wise"—or more subtly with the choice of adjectives or adverbs, value-loaded comments that clearly implied the opinion that an author intended for his readers to share—"It was a terrible accident," "He acted rashly," etc. Gertrude Stein was experimenting with sentence structure and word repetitions, trying to immerse her readers in a sense of an ongoing present, and achieving a poetic quality through her repetitions that focused attention on certain words and their meanings. Sherwood Anderson, like Joyce, wrote stories in which the plot was not everything: the stories, like those of O. Henry, did not snap shut at the end with a clever click, thus exhibiting the author's ingenuity. Instead, the stories developed gradually, seemingly aimlessly, their intent being a revelation of character or of a way of life. All three authors defined character less through authorial description and more through what a character said and did. Obviously none of these techniques are entirely new to the twentieth century, but the extent to which these authors used them was.

In poetry, Ezra Pound was reacting against the metronomic beat of Victorian poetry, a heavily cadenced style, of Charles Swinburne, for example, where the sound lulled one into inattention to meaning. Pound's credo was "Make it new." His technique insisted that writers:

Use no superfluous word, no adjective which does not reveal something.
Don't use such an expression as "dim lands of *peace*." It dulls the image. It mixes an abstraction with the concrete. It comes from the writer's not realizing the natural object is always the *adequate* symbol.
Go in fear of abstractions.[1]

In part the period's style was a natural reaction to overblown Victorian rhetoric, but after World War I that reaction was intensified by a distrust of language itself, caused by the heavy use of propaganda by both sides during the war. If words like *honor, duty, noble and sacred purpose* could be used to get young men to kill one another merely to extend economic spheres of influence or to play age-old political games, then language itself was suspect, and modernist writers experimented with a variety of new forms. One was an insistence on objectivity, a precise detailing of concrete objects, allowing readers to make their own conclusions; this insistence on objectivity is what Pound refers to when he says "go in fear of abstractions" and use the natural object as symbol.

Hemingway knew and studied with each of the writers above: Pound, Anderson, Stein, and Joyce. Their influence accentuated the spare, laconic style he had already developed in high school, under the influence of naturalist writer Jack London and sports writer and satirist Ring Lardner; Hemingway's style was honed at the *Kansas City Star,* pared still further by a foreign correspondent's need to cable stories back in condensed form. But the spare, unadorned, grammatically simple, declarative sentences, largely devoid of adjective or adverb, also echoed Hemingway's own philosophy. He modified sportswriter Grantland Rice's "not that you won or lost, but how you played the game," to a belief that since one always lost, the only thing that mattered was how one played, how one conducted oneself. For Hemingway, loss was inevitable: fate, circumstance, something always saw to it that what one wanted, one could not keep. We might find love, but the love expired or the person we loved died. Later he expressed this pessimistic belief in *Death in the Afternoon:*

All stories, if continued far enough, end in death, and he is no true-story teller who would keep that from you. Especially do all stories of monogamy end in death, and your man who is monogamous while he often lives most happily, dies in the most lonely fashion. . . . If two people love each other there can be no happy end to it. (p. 122)

Similarly, one might find fame, but it would either be evanescent or its own punishment. And since one cannot control fate, since one is bound to lose, one should maintain one's dignity and control one's own response to losing. This personal philosophy, sometimes referred to in criticism as "the Hemingway code," is both stoic and existential: one should not complain, one should show "grace under pressure" (Hemingway's definition of courage); but also, one should care about one's craft, one's method and style in playing the game, since an individual's choices and actions defined him or her.

In *Death in the Afternoon*, Hemingway recounts his attempts at learning to write well in Paris:

I was trying to write then and I found the greatest difficulty, aside from knowing truly what you really felt, rather than what you were supposed to feel, and had been taught to feel, was to put down what really happened in action; what the actual things were which produced the emotion that you experienced. . . . [I was trying to get] the real thing, the sequence of motion and fact which made the emotion.   (p. 2)

One sees the reporter trying to describe what happened (not always what "really" happened, since much of what he recounts is fictional), but to separate out his own emotions and yet describe a scene, "a sequence of motion and fact" in such a way that it would produce emotion in the reader without editorial intrusion on the author's part.

The vignettes of *in our time* show this process well. The following, based on dispatches he sent the Toronto *Star* and published there in October 1922, but reworked and condensed still more for his book, describes the evacuation of Greek nationals west through Thrace ahead of invading Turkish troops.

Minarets stuck up in the rain out of Adrianople across the mud flats. The carts were jammed for thirty miles along the Karagatch road. Water buffalo and camel were hauling carts through the mud. There was no end and no beginning. Just carts loaded with everything they owned. The old men and women, soaked through, walked along keeping the cattle moving. The Maritza was running yellow almost up to the bridge. Carts were jammed solid on the bridge with camels bobbing along through them. Greek cavalry herded along the procession. The women and children were in the carts, crouched with mattresses, mirrors, sewing machines, bundles. There was a woman having a baby with a young girl holding a blanket over her and crying. Scared sick looking at it. It rained all through the evacuation. ("Chapter 2," *In Our Time*)

Minarets, water buffalo, and camels establish the exotic locale, and the mass retreat indicates that the minarets, and the religion that they stand for, are insufficient sanctuary for the refugees. *They* in the fifth sentence has no grammatical referent, creating the sense of confusion and impersonality, a sense heightened by the verb *herded,* applied to the refugees, depersonalizing them. The only editorial comment is "There was no end and no beginning," but it is unobtrusive. Hemingway nowhere says that the men are not present because they are away at war; that is implicit. Nor does he plead for the reader's sympathy. If this "sequence of motion and fact" cannot convey the plight of the refugees, then anything else would only be spurious. Note too that in this brief paragraph describing one incident, Hemingway includes the entire cycle of life and death, birth, flight, and war, in rain and mud. Existence can be terrible, and the bare facts, seemingly barely presented, are sufficient to convey that.

A cycle of birth and death, similar to the vignette of the refugees fleeing Adrianople, occurs in the short story "Indian Camp" in *In Our Time*, Hemingway's first Nick Adams story.[2] Nick is an adolescent in "Indian Camp" and in "The Doctor and the Doctor's Wife," has broken up with his girl friend in "The End of Something," has left home in "The Battler," is wounded in the war in vignette "Chapter 6," all of *In Our Time,* and by the end of *Winner Take Nothing* is himself the father of an adolescent boy. Since his father is a doctor, since he fishes in northern Michigan, and since the reader watches him grow up, mature, go to war and return, he seems like, and has been interpreted as, a fictional portrait of the author, comparable to Joyce's *Portrait of the Artist as a Young Man* and Anderson's *Winesburg, Ohio. In Our Time* draws its title, ironically, from the

Book of Common Prayer's plea, "give us peace in our time, Lord"; ironic, since the book portrays war between nations and strife between individuals, and even within them. Many of Hemingway's stories, certainly the Nick Adams ones, are tales of initiation, accounts of rites of passage or of epiphanies, awarenesses on the protagonist's part as to the nature of existence.

In "Indian Camp," Dr. Henry Adams is called while on vacation to assist an Indian woman in labor; he takes with him to the Indians' camp his brother George and his son Nick, who is too young to leave alone. It is a breech birth, and the doctor must perform a caesarean section. Not having his medical bag with him on vacation, he performs the operation without anesthetic, using his jackknife and suturing the wound with fishing leader, with Nick as his assistant, holding a basin for the afterbirth. When the doctor sews up the incision, "Nick did not watch. His curiosity had been gone for a long time" (*In Our Time*, p. 19). Hemingway's extreme understatement, though flatly stated, implies how traumatic the scene has been for the young boy.

During the operation, the woman's husband, who had cut his foot badly with an ax three days before, lay in an upper bunk above his wife. He has had to listen to her scream through two days of protracted labor without being able to help, his impotence signaled by his wound. He cannot ease his wife's pain, cannot relieve her agony. That he is a member of an oppressed minority, living in abject poverty as a bark-peeler, adds to his impotence, as does the very slight suggestion that the infant is not his child, but George's (who passes out cigars and who has his arm bitten during the delivery, a bite suggestive of passion). Unable to endure his own inability, the husband quietly commits suicide, slitting his throat, and Nick sees the result.

At story's end, Nick and his father return across the lake from the darkness, the trauma, of the Indian camp.

The sun was coming up over the hills. A bass jumped, making a circle in the water. Nick trailed his hand in the water. It felt warm in the sharp chill of the morning.

In the early morning on the lake sitting in the stern of the boat with his father rowing, he felt quite sure that he would never die. (*In Our Time* p. 21)

As Pound had said, "the natural object is always the *adequate* symbol." Nick, as a child, is still in his morning. He has experienced a circle—birth and death, light and darkness, warmth and cold. He has learned that both life and death can be brutal, ugly. His innocence has been assaulted, but as the last sentence indicates, he still is secure in the presence of his father and his youthful illusions, including that of his own immortality.

In "The Doctor and the Doctor's Wife," Doctor Adams is confronted with an awareness of his own lack of control and cowardice and with repeated evidence of his wife's lack of understanding. The doctor has asked an Indian indebted to him for medical services to cut up some logs that have washed ashore, logs that may or may not have been abandoned by lumber companies. To evade the work, or to establish his own equality with the superior doctor, the Indian calls the logs stolen, and Doctor Adams loses his temper and threatens the Indian, a challenge the doctor then backs away from. At his summer cottage, his wife waits in darkness, "the blinds drawn." She is a Christian Scientist who believes that only the Lord heals, not doctors like her husband. Nor does she believe that anyone would avoid payment of a debt or start an argument to do so: "Dear, I don't think, I really don't think that any one would really do a thing like that." Hemingway's repetition of her "I don't think" characterizes her naïveté. The doctor, to compensate for his furious impotence, plays with his shotgun. Although young Nick does not witness either scene, he must choose between his parents, the implication being that the divergent values and tensions between the parents have been visited on their son; that their misunderstandings echo those of the entire book, a world of violence and insecurity into which a young man growing up must be initiated.

The last story in the volume appears in two parts and was at that time Hemingway's longest piece of writing. It admirably exhibits Hemingway's "iceberg technique": "There is seven-eighths of [an iceberg] underwater for every part that shows. Anything you know you can eliminate and it only strengthens your iceberg."[3] "Big Two-Hearted River" is a story of Nick's return, after being wounded, from World War I, seeking recuperation, a form of recreational therapy, in nature. The submerged iceberg, as Hemingway says in A Moveable Feast (p. 77) is that the war is never mentioned, but there are distinct clues to it. First, "River" occurs at the end of In Our Time, after we have read of Nick's wounding, and Nick is still wearing a khaki shirt. Second, the burned-over landscape of Seney is a "natural object" that easily suggests the landscape of war, as the sooty grasshopper suggests Nick's own condition in trying to readjust: "He realized that the fire must have come the year before, but the grasshoppers were all black now. He wondered how long they would stay that way" (p. 181). Hemingway, in this story, is not explicit as to the site of the wound; we do not know if Nick is still recovering from a physical wound—no physical limitations are mentioned— or from the trauma of being wounded, of having his immortality shattered. Nick is mentally very shaky, and, again, a natural symbol conveys his need for stability: He "watched the trout keeping themselves steady in the current with wavering fins"; "He watched them holding themselves with their noses into the current" (p. 177). In coming to nature, and in occupying himself with physical tasks, Nick "felt he had left everything behind, the need for thinking" (p. 179).[4]

Nick's mental instability is subtly conveyed. Having lost a fish, "He felt, vaguely, a little sick, as though it would be better to sit down" (p. 204). His reaction far exceeds the cause; fishermen lose trout often without becoming nauseous or dizzy. Similarly, Nick's recuperative efforts can be missed by the inattentive reader. After hiking into the back country and setting up his camp, Nick muses: "Now things were done. There had been this to do. Now it was done. It had been a hard trip. He was very tired. That was done. He had made his camp" (p. 186), and so forth. Even for Hemingway, these sentences are very short. They convey the instability of a man who must focus on doing so that he does not think, on the exhausted mental state of a man who must concentrate on the task at hand lest the mind wander, ask unanswerable questions (Why me?), and become unmanageable. Occupational therapy provides simple, do-able tasks to practice coordination and to build confidence: "He drove [a nail] into the pine tree, holding it close and hitting it gently with the flat of the ax. He hung the pack up on the nail. All his supplies were in the pack. They were off the ground and sheltered now" (p. 187).

Having set up a comfortable camp, Nick does think, remembering nostalgically, knowing himself to be tired enough to go to sleep when he wants to. The next day, he does catch fish, and the therapy proceeds well. Down river, the future, is a tangled swamp. "Nick did not want to go in there now. . . . He did not want to go down stream any further today" (p. 211). The future is still uncertain, but the present, in its ambiguities, has been masterfully presented by Hemingway, who suggests Nick's predicament with artistic understatement and without authorial editorializing.

Hemingway began writing the manuscript of what would become *The Sun Also Rises* on his twenty-sixth birthday, in July 1925, and finished the first draft on September 21.[5] Then, excited by his accomplishment, he felt as he describes Dr. Adams's state after the successful caesarean in "Indian Camp": "He was feeling exalted and talkative as football players are in a dressing room after a game." In his exhuberance, he wrote a parody of Sherwood Anderson's recent novel *Dark Laughter* and submitted the parody to his and Anderson's publisher, Boni and Liveright, guessing correctly that they would reject a book that would hold up to ridicule their leading author; thus Hemingway freed himself from his contract with them. The parody, *The Torrents of Spring,* is his most openly literary book. It takes its title from the Russian author Ivan Turgenev, its chapter epigraphs from English author Henry Fielding, its subject matter and style from Anderson, and like Anderson's book, it alludes to numerous contemporary authors (including Gertrude Stein, John Dos Passos, and F. Scott Fitzgerald, whom

Hemingway describes as drunk). The parody is accurate, and for one chapter might be funny, but aside from the lack of kindness in pillorying friends, the humor is too much of an in joke to be long sustained, and it quickly palls.

The Sun Also Rises has two epigraphs: one from Gertrude Stein about "the lost generation," one from the Biblical book Ecclesiastes about the abiding earth, a passage that also provides the novel with its title. Stein had had difficulty getting her car repaired, and a French garage owner complained to her about the young men of the war generation as "lost," irresponsible and untrainable, a comment Stein repeated to Hemingway. He balanced her denunciation with the permanence of nature, as demonstrated in "Big Two-Hearted River." Generations may come and go, but nature lasts, and so do certain values.

The novel continues to investigate impotence, already examined in "Indian Camp" and "The Doctor and the Doctor's Wife," as well as other stories in *In Our Time*.[6] One aspect of realism, in contrast to romanticism, was that individuals were depicted not as the masters of their fate, but rather as without control over their destiny, and *The Sun Also Rises* is a distinctly antiromantic novel. Its first-person narrator is Jake Barnes, an American newspaper correspondent in Paris, who was injured in a plane crash in World War I: his penis was damaged, but not his testicles; Jake has normal sexual desires, but is incapable of satisfying them. (This is all implicit, like the iceberg, but there is a poignant scene where Jake surveys the damage in a mirror beside his bed and then cries himself to sleep [pp. 30–31].)

Jake is contrasted to Robert Cohn, son of wealthy parents, outsider as Jew, former middleweight boxing champion of Princeton, novelist, and—one might say, very preppy—Hemingway says foolishly governed by an outmoded, impractical, romantic code. Cohn believes much of what he reads, from H. L. Mencken's opinion of Paris, rather than his own experience, to guidebook descriptions of Spanish architecture. His most disruptive romantic belief is that, in the twentieth century, casual sex is identical with love, and that his brief affair with Lady Brett Ashley amounts, on her part, to the lifelong commitment he would like it to be. Thus, he follows Brett and her fiancé Michael around, even though he is told he isn't wanted, unable to reconcile his belief that sex equals love with Brett's indifference. Cohn loves the fictions of W. H. Hudson, and believing them, wants to visit South America. Jake mocks this aspect of Cohn: "For a man to take [Hudson's novel] at thirty-four as a guide-book to what life holds is about as safe as it would be for a man of the same age to enter Wall Street direct from a French convent, equipped with a complete set of the more practical Alger books" (p. 9). Hemingway also mocks other romantic writings: Jake, while fishing, reads a story of a woman whose husband falls into a glacial crevasse, and who waits twenty-four years for the glacier to deposit him; Jake and his friend Bill, on their fishing trip, visit the monastery of Roncevaux, where the knight Roland, hero of the French epic poem the *Chanson de Roland,* fought a tragic rearguard action against the Saracens on Charlemagne's behalf. Hemingway's point, which reiterates his philosophy, is that right does not always triumph, wickedness is not always punished; God's not in His heaven and all's not right with the world. The romantic world is over, and so are romantic codes. Cohn is foolish for wanting to punch Jake for offhandedly saying "go to hell."

> He stood up from the table his face white, and stood there white and angry behind the hors d'oeuvres.
> "Sit down," I said. "Don't be a fool."
> "You've got to take that back."
> "Oh, cut out the prep school stuff." (p. 39)

Cohn is equally foolish wanting to fight to defend the honor of Lady Ashley, who has the title by marriage but is no traditional lady.

Brett Ashley is very much a twentieth-century woman. She drinks at least as much as the men do (she may well be an alcoholic) and sleeps around as any man might. Her "own true love had . . . kicked off with the dysentery" dur-

ing the war, and on the rebound she had married Lord Ashley, who slept with a loaded revolver, threatened Brett with
it, and made her sleep on the floor (p. 203). Her wartime
service was as a nurse's aide, which is how she met Jake. In
the course of the novel, she sleeps with Cohn, her fiancé
Michael Campbell, and the bullfighter Pedro Romero, but
she loves Jake, with whom sex is impossible; it is implied
that they have tried to live together to their mutual frustra-
tion. In conservative, Catholic, mid-1920s Spain, Brett runs
around with mannish short hair, without stockings, in
men's hats, calling herself and her male friends "chaps."
Spanish dancers at the bullfighting festival of San Fermin
dance around her, making of her an object of veneration,
similar to the images of the church, a fertility figure. But
Hemingway has borrowed imagery from T. S. Eliot's poem
The Waste Land, and his expatriates inhabit a world
largely devoid of spiritual values: his Paris and Spain are no
paradises, and Brett is no fertility goddess, although Jake
may be both questing knight and Fisher King.[7]

The novel, in realistic fashion, seems plotless and episodic
(people's lives do not have the dramatic unity that a play-
wright could give them). Jake begins his memoir in Paris,
introducing us to Robert Cohn, Brett, Michael, and another
friend and writer, Bill Gorton, who has come from America
on vacation. After some partying in Paris, Jake and Bill go
to Spain for fishing, then on to the festival of San Fermin at
Pamplona for the bullfighting, where they are reunited with
Brett, Mike, and Robert, and do more drinking. At the fiesta, they meet, and Brett falls in love with, the nineteen-
year-old bullfighter, Romero, and she spends a night with
him. The sexual jealousy that has been building up between
Mike and Robert finally explodes. Cohn knocks down Jake
and Mike, finds Brett in Romero's bedroom, and savagely
beats up the young bullfighter. Romero, however, refuses
Cohn's apology, hits Cohn whenever Robert comes near
him (Romero is sitting on the floor unable to get up), and
threatens to kill Cohn in the morning if Cohn is still in
town. Cohn does leave, sadder if not wiser. The fiesta concludes with the last day of the bullfight (*The Sun Also Rises*

was published in England as *Fiesta*), and then Brett leaves
Pamplona for Madrid with Romero. Jake goes to the coast
to recuperate from his vacation, where a telegram from
Brett comes saying that she is alone in Madrid, having convinced Romero that she will be no good for him. Jake takes
the train to her, and, as always in her presence, near the one
he loves but cannot have, be begins drinking heavily again.
The novel concludes with Brett saying, "Oh, Jake, . . . we
could have had such a damned good time together," if only
he had not been wounded. Jake replies, "Yes, . . . isn't it
pretty to think so?," signaling his recognition that it is not
his wound alone that prevents true and blissful love between them.

Mike Campbell, like Brett, Jake, and Bill, is hard-
drinking; he is also an undischarged bankrupt, living on an
allowance from his wealthy mother. As Hemingway uses
Jake's impotence metaphorically, so does he with Mike's
bankruptcy. All the expatriates in the novel are deraci-
nated—uprooted from home, country, and former values—
by the war and its aftermath. They no longer can depend
on such outmoded codes as romanticism, nor on organized
religion to solve their problems (it neither prevented the
war—both sides prayed to the same God—nor does it relieve Jake's misery over his wound and inability to have
Brett). These codes are impotent, bankrupt. Thus the reader
sees Jake seeking for a new code, one empirically, induc-
tively developed that will enable him to cope in an absurd
world, in contrast to Cohn, who follows an archaic code,
and in contrast to ill-mannered Mike. Mike's state of bankruptcy, as I have said, has its behavioral aspects; so does
Mike's declaration that "I never play games, even" (p. 191).
Social self-control—not complaining before others, bearing
one's grief stoically, maintaining one's dignity, acting with
good manners—is a form of a game.

Another individual the reader meets in Paris is Count Mippipopolous, who also pursues Brett, but who, when she
declines his advances, behaves courteously and with self-
control, unlike Cohn, even driving Brett to Jake's apartment
and taking them both out to dinner. The count has suffered

through seven wars and four revolutions; he is, as Brett says, "one of us" (the phrase comes from Conrad's *Lord Jim*). As with Jake, his wartime experience has brought him pain, self-knowledge, and wisdom: "You see . . . , it is because I have lived very much that now I can enjoy everything so well. . . . You must get to know the values." Or as Jake says later, "Perhaps as you went along you did learn something. . . . Maybe if you found out how to live in it you learned from that what it was all about" (p. 148).

One role model for Jake is Count Mippipopolous; another is Pedro Romero. Like the count, but unlike Jake, Michael, and Robert, Romero maintains his dignity in the presence of Brett. He desires her, but will not make a fool of himself for her. He possesses the quality Jakes strives for, immense self-control (even to the unrealistic point of not allowing himself to be knocked out by the superior boxer, Cohn). He fights close to the bull, less to court the danger than to heighten his art of bullfighting. Even bruised and beaten by Cohn, he controls his body; given a bull with defective vision, he uses his skill to bring the best out of the animal, while making a gift of the performance to Brett and still maintaining his own individuality:

Everything of which he could control the locality he did in front of her all that afternoon. Never once did he look up. He made it stronger that way, and did it for himself, too, as well her. Because he did not look up to ask if it pleased he did it all for himself inside, and it strengthened him, and yet he did it for her, too.[8] (p. 216)

For Hemingway, bullfighting is a complex of many things. It is a ritual drama, a tragedy, in which spectators can vicariously share in a life-and-death struggle; and, as in a Greek tragedy, the purging of their emotions (cf. *The Sun Also Rises* p. 164). It is an athletic contest, in which the matador holds off death for a little while, and thus it serves as a wished-for microcosm of life, where death cannot be forestalled. (Although *The Sun Also Rises* is antiromantic, Hemingway himself is frequently romantic, which is part of the reason why he can portray Cohn so realistically and sympathetically.) Bullfighting is also an aesthetic spectacle, performance art where one's life depends on one's performance, and thus an equivalent for the way in which one should conduct one's life: with skill, courage, self-control, and dignity. Thus Romero, who possesses these virtues, becomes a code hero whom Jake, the protagonist, seeks to emulate; and *The Sun Also Rises* is a novel about the wasteland of the postwar world and about injured, impotent Jake's quest for appropriate values and a feasible code of conduct. Michael Reynolds suggests that it is also Jake's confession for having failed to live up to his own code.[9]

The Sun Also Rises is generally acknowledged to be Hemingway's best novel. Although he began the book calling the narrator Hem and the other characters by their real names, in the course of writing he distanced himself from his protagonist, combined characters, condensed events and invented others, and taught himself the art of novel writing. The book works on a number of levels. It does present implicit criticism of the hedonistic, amoral life-style of the expatriates, as it was originally received by some critics. It does present a lively picture of Paris and Pamplona during the Roaring Twenties, a picture of dissolute life sharply and accurately rendered, one that influenced young people following publication. But it also presents Jake's spiritual struggle (he is named for the Biblical Jacob, who wrestled with an angel and was, unlike Jake Barnes, the father of a tribe). And it accomplishes all with a hard-edged prose style that demands reader involvement while subtly conveying the author's intentions. Consider the following passages, the first of which describes the removal of a dead bull from the bullfight arena.

They had hitched the mules to the dead bull and then the whips cracked, the men ran, and the mules, straining forward, their legs pushing, broke into a gallop, and the bull, one horn up, his head on its side swept a swath smoothly across the sand and out the red gate. (pp. 168–69)

I have italicized the *d*s that signal past participle, death, and completion. The multiplicity of commas together with the glottal stops (the closure of the air passage in the throat after hard consonants), causes the first half of the sentence to read jerkily, gaining momentum (appropriately) with *ran*, which ends with a nasal consonant, not a hard stop, increasing that momentum with the present participles, until the bull, like the sentence, flows smoothly along. The "red gate," however, brings us and the sentence to a halt, with its suggestion of death. At the novel's first bullfight, Jake says:

I sat beside Brett and explained to Brett what it was all about ... so that it became more something that was going on with a definite end, and less of a spectacle with unexplained horrors. I had her watch how Romero took the bull away from a fallen horse with his cape, and how he held him with the cape and turned him smoothly and suavely, never wasting the bull.

... Romero never made any contortions, always it was straight and pure and natural in line.   (p. 168)

As Jake himself has tried to figure "what it was all about" (p. 148), so he tries to explain to Brett the bloody spectacle they are witnessing so that the violence will seem less absurd, as it does in life, and more meaningful in the ritual of the bullfight. Hemingway's prose matches the rhythms and smoothness of Romero's capework, again emphasizing the ongoing action with present participles and a more than usual amount of adverbs. Finally, there is a self-reflexive quality to the description: Hemingway is trying to achieve what he praises Romero for accomplishing, the creation of a "straight and pure and natural" line, all the while eschewing overt judgment of the characters, leaving all such evaluations to the reader. The novel's ambiguities demand close reading and rereadings, and the interpretations are not yet done.

3

To the Pinnacle of Success and Beyond

Hemingway's next volume of short stories, *Men Without Women* (1927), the title expressing both a thematic concern of the stories and the author's condition between wives at the time that many of the stories were written, continues his high level of achievement from *In Our Time* and *The Sun Also Rises.* Particularly good are "The Undefeated," "In Another Country," "Hills Like White Elephants," and "The Killers." "The Killers," for many years Hemingway's most anthologized short story, is another tale in the initiation and maturation of Nick Adams.[1] A still-youthful Nick—he reacts to being tied and gagged as an adventure—encounters two Chicago hit men who have come to a small-town diner, seeking to kill a boxer who has double-crossed the mob and is fleeing its vengeance. When the boxer, Ole Andreson, does not show up for dinner, the killers leave, and Nick goes to warn him, only to discover that the boxer is tired of running and will neither appeal to the police for help nor leave town. Andreson made his choice and now must live or die by it; he is resigned to his fate. Nick, still young and full of romantic idealism, is appalled. Life should be susceptible of emendation, but he learns that it isn't always. All that Nick can do is leave town, which will not protect his life from evil, or "not think about it" (p. 289), which did not work for Jake Barnes. The killers are not big men, but small and overdressed, appearing like vaudeville comedians; evil does not always announce itself as such. Similarly, the woman who runs Mrs. Hirsch's rooming house is not Mrs. Hirsch, but Mrs. Bell, who thinks that Mr. Andreson should not stay in his room but should take a walk outside on such a nice fall day. Subtly, quietly, Hemingway insists that the world is not as we superficially perceive it to be.

"In Another Country" (which takes its title from Christopher Marlowe's *The Jew of Malta* by way of T. S. Eliot's "Portrait of a Lady") is told by an unnamed American narrator, who might easily be Nick Adams, in Milan in World War I. Like Hemingway, the narrator has suffered a leg wound and is undergoing physical therapy on machines designed to strengthen his leg. Beside him is an Italian major, a former fencing champion, undergoing treatment of his crippled hand. The major insists that the narrator speak correct grammar, learn Italian properly, play by all the rules, as he has, as fencer, as soldier, and as man, waiting until he was invalided out of the war to marry so as not to chance leaving a young bride a widow. But like the physical therapy machines, which do little good, the conventional rules don't work: the major's bride dies of pneumonia. Not just war, life itself is absurd.

"The Undefeated" is a story about a craftsman and artist, a bullfighter named Manuel Garcia.[2] Again, Hemingway uses the matador as an embodiment of someone dedicated to an art, who practices that skill to the very best of his ability, in spite of the bad luck that continually besets him. His skill and dedication define him, in contrast to a newspaper critic who uses stale clichés, and who is willing to leave the arena and write his report for his evening paper based, not on the actual fight, but on the reviews from the morning papers. Garcia, no longer young, has just emerged from the hospital following a goring; the only bullfight he can obtain is an evening fight, as a replacement, for less wages than he is worth; for the bullfight promoter, bullfighting is a business, with a profit to be made, unsentimentally. For him, it is not an art. A friend tries to talk Manuel out of returning to the ring, at his age, and in his condition, but Garcia defines himself as a bullfighter. He fights well that evening, but he has very bad luck—like Jake, like the

Italian major—and cannot kill the bull cleanly. (In his bull-fighting book, *Death in the Afternoon,* Hemingway insists upon the need for luck in killing cleanly and expeditiously.) Garcia trips on debris thrown by an unsympathetic crowd, and is gored once more. The title of the story anticipates a line from *The Old Man and the Sea;* that "a man can be destroyed but not defeated." Fate, circumstance, bad luck can ruin what one has striven for. As Robert Frost put it:

Three foggy mornings and one rainy day
Will rot the best birch fence a man can build.   ("Home Burial")

Garcia is destroyed, but not defeated; he knows that he fought well, and he refuses to allow his pigtail, which marks him as a matador, to be cut away. He measures himself by professional standards, his own and those of Zurito, the picador, and that is all that matters to him, not the opinion of the ignorant crowd. Hemingway clearly admires Garcia, but he raises an issue that he will deal with at more length later in his career: when is bravery and dedication to a cause indistinguishable from foolishness and foolhardiness?

"Hills Like White Elephants" is one of Hemingway's best short stories. An admirable example of both the iceberg technique and the absence of authorial intrusion, it captures a brief scene in the lives of two people, an unremarkable scene that unmistakably discloses the rupture of a close relationship. The story is set at a railway stop, a juncture, in the Ebro Valley of Spain. On one side the Ebro is dry, sterile: "There was no shade and no trees and the station was between two lines of rails in the sun" (p. 273); on the other side "were fields of grain and trees along the banks of the Ebro" (p. 276). The couple, never named (except the nickname Jig for the woman), are also between two positions, one of fertility, one of sterility—continued closeness and joy, or misunderstanding and separation. Their discussion centers around an operation for the woman, never named, but obviously an abortion. (One must remember that the setting for the story is Catholic, conservative Spain of the 1920s: abortions are illegal, condemned by the church, difficult to obtain, and dangerous.)

The man selfishly wants the woman to himself and does not want the child to come between them. (The story never makes clear whether they are married or not.)

> "It's really an awfully simple operation, Jig," the man said.
> ... "We'll be fine afterward. Just like we were before."
> "What makes you think so?"
> "That's the only thing that bothers us. It's the only thing that's made us unhappy." (p. 275)

The woman is obviously torn between her desire to have their child and to maintain the relationship, and the man cannot see beyond his own desires to empathize with her; their views are like the train tracks, parallel but never meeting. Other symbolic barriers in the story include that of language—Spanish, that the woman doesn't speak, but even in English she and the man are not speaking the same language, not communicating—the glass beads that screen the bar, and the hills like white elephants. White elephants are, of course, unwanted objects, something to be gotten rid of. Regardless of their decision, their relationship has reached a juncture. If the woman consents to the abortion, it will affect her emotionally—it already has—and she will resent the man's forcing her into it. If she does not, the man will resent her and the child. Unless the man changes his entire personality and accepts the child, an unlikely event, it is a no-win situation, sketched in suggestive outline by a consummate artist.

Although the story is an everyday one of conflicting desires within a relationship and of lack of understanding, it is obvious that the narrator's sympathies are with the woman. After the man has carried their luggage around the station to the proper track, he goes inside for a drink: "He drank an Anis at the bar and looked at the people. They were all waiting reasonably for the train" (p. 277–78).

Here Hemingway shifts from third-person objective to the man's point of view: "reasonably" is the man's opinion. Because he has not been privy to the conversations at the bar, the quiet people seem reasonable to him, in contrast to Jig. But it is not unreasonable to question an abortion. Insofar as the conflict needs a villain, the man in the story is it, and Hemingway's depiction of the woman's plight, and that of the situation in its entirety, is sensitive and understanding. Nevertheless, from Virginia Woolf's review of *Men Without Women*[3] through the present, Hemingway has been the target of feminist critics who frequently condemn the writer for the behavior of both his characters and himself, not as artist, but as macho soldier, lion hunter, and four-times-married man. In "Hills Like White Elephants," and in "Up in Michigan," the sympathies of the narrator are clearly with the woman character and her plight; the depiction of the males shows them to be self-centered and lacking understanding. It may well be that Hemingway was accurately describing aspects of his own behavior in his fiction, but the artist should not be reviled for the accuracy of his depiction of real-life situations, nor should he be confused with his fictional characters.

Two years later, Hemingway scored an even greater success among the critics and the general public with the publication of his second novel, *A Farewell to Arms* (1929), another first-person narrative. The title comes from George Peele's Renaissance poem of the same title, as it was anthologized in Hemingway's day (now the poem is collected as "The Old Knight" or known from its first line: "His golden locks time hath to silver turned"), about Queen Elizabeth's champion retiring from martial combat; the title also puns on the opening line of Virgil's *Aeneid:* "I sing of arms and the man." In Hemingway's novel, his protagonist, Frederic Henry, bids farewell to both the armaments of war and the arms of his beloved, Catherine Barkley.

Frederic (no *k*, named by Hemingway at least partly for the foolish protagonist of Flaubert's *A Sentimental Education*) is an ambulance driver, not with the Red Cross, but as a lieutenant in the Italian Army in northeastern Italy. The novel begins in the fall of 1915 with a scene of domesticity among the soldiers at war, the first chapter containing two often-cited descriptions:

The vineyards were thin and bare-branched too and all the country wet and brown and dead with the autumn. . . . And the troops were muddy and wet in their capes; their rifles were wet and under their capes the two leather cartridge-boxes on the front of the belts, gray leather boxes heavy with the packs of clips of thin, long 6.5 mm. cartridges, bulged forward under the capes so that the men, passing on the road, marched as though they were six months gone with child. (p. 4)

Again, the scenery sets the tone of sterility and death, reinforced by the image of the soldiers, pregnant with death. The chapter concludes:

At the start of the winter came the permanent rain and with the rain came the cholera. But it was checked and in the end only seven thousand died of it in the army. (p. 4)

How many may have died of cholera outside the army is immaterial to a military man, although it is known that well over ten million died of influenza during the war, but the irony of *only* seven thousand deaths is obvious.

Henry takes an extended leave the following year during the winter rains, and the company priest urges Henry to visit his (the priest's) hometown high in the mountains, where the air is clear and dry "and it is understood that a man may love God. It is not a dirty joke" (p. 71). Hemingway has, as Carlos Baker first noted, created a contrast between the mountains, where things are cleaner, purer, and the valleys and plains with their moral sinkholes. The soldiers in Henry's company shuttle back and forth between whorehouse and combat, deriding the priest, accusing him of masturbation and of wanting the war to continue. Hemingway thus offers Henry moral choices, but Frederic spends his leave drinking and whoring at various fleshpots in Italy, no higher than the seven hills of Rome, although remorseful about his choices.

On his return, he is disappointed to discover that the war, and his ambulances, functioned as usual without his presence; more pleasantly, he meets Catherine Barkley, a British nurse's aide. Catherine is obviously mentally unstable: she has been nursing at the bloody French front for over a year, and her fiancé was blown up in the Battle of the Somme the previous year. Now she is nursing in Italy, where she doesn't speak the language, and where—so as not to tempt the Italian troops too grievously—the British nurses are largely restricted to quarters. She is tall, and very beautiful, with long, blonde hair, and gray eyes. Henry determines to make a sexual conquest:

Catherine: "You did say you loved me, didn't you?"
Frederic: "Yes," I lied. "I love you." I had not said it before.
. . . I thought she was probably a little crazy. It was all right if she was. I did not care what I was getting into. This was better than going every evening to the house for officers where the girls climbed all over you and put your cap on backward as a sign of affection between their trips upstairs with brother officers. I knew I did not love Catherine Barkley nor had any idea of loving her. This was a game. (p. 30)

Soon after, while waiting to evacuate wounded troops and while eating dinner, Henry is struck, as Hemingway had been, by a trench mortar shell and is returned to Milan for surgery and recuperation; Catherine is transferred to his hospital, and there, before his surgery, with his wounded legs in bandages, goes to bed with him for the first time (unrealistic, but romantic). And Henry learns that it isn't mere sex for him any longer: he loves Catherine. There is an extended period of recuperation, during which Catherine becomes pregnant, and Henry returns to his unit in the fall of 1917, in time for the Italian retreat from Caporetto.

His assignment is to take three ambulances loaded with medical supplies from Gorizia to Pordenone, but because the main roads are stalled with retreating troop convoys and refugees, Henry tries to move his ambulances by back roads, and gets them stuck in the mud. Abandoning them, he tries to take his three men around invading German forces at Udine, where one of his men is killed. At the Tagliamento River, Italian troops are screening retreaters for those speaking Italian with an accent (as Fred Henry does), possible German spies, and shooting officers for allowing their men to retreat. A sure victim on both scores, Henry dives into the river and deserts, like Nick Adams of Chapter 6 of *In Our Time,* making "a separate peace"; eventually he makes his way back to Milan.

Catherine is vacationing at Stresa on Lago Maggiore, on the Italian border, and Henry, out of uniform now, joins her there. Informed that he will be arrested as a deserter, he rows Catherine the length of the lake at night (along with swimming clothed in the Tagliamento, Henry's only acts of physical prowess) to the neutral country of Switzerland. There they await the end of the war and the birth of their child, walking, playing cards, reading. Catherine's labor is protracted, a caesarean is necessitated, but the baby is born dead, strangled by the umbilicus, and Catherine dies of hemorrhages. As with the stories of *In Our Time,* Hemingway insists that both war and life are absurd and tragic:

If people bring so much courage to this world, the world has to kill them to break them, so of course it kills them. The world breaks every one and afterward many are strong at the broken places. But those that will not break it kills. (p. 249)

That was what you did. You died. You did not know what it was about. You never had time to learn. They threw you in and told you the rules and the first time they caught you off base they killed you. (p. 327)

Although the love story adds poignancy to the war story, both end unexpectedly and tragically. At the beginning of the novel, Henry has told Catherine he never loved anyone, and he tells the priest, "I don't love." Since Frederic is so unheroic, so selfish initially, he is an unusual hero. Jake Barnes has prepared us for unheroic protagonists: Jake doesn't win the girl, gets punched out by Cohn, but Jake is more likable than Frederic, certainly worthy of more sympathy. Jake at least takes charge of many situations. Fred is often inept. Questioned as to why he received a medal for his wounding, "Did you do any heroic act?" Fred replies, "No. ... I was blown up while we were eating cheese." Other than hedonism and a care to perform his duty, he has no philosophy (or even the attempt at fashioning one that one sees Jake undergoing), no rationale for being in the war on the Italian side, with no concern at first for anyone but himself.

Catherine, who has suffered more initially than he has, gives herself to him, knowing that at first it is just a sexual game for him. She commits herself to him romantically, and in doing so commits herself back to life, painful though it may be. Like Manuel Garcia, she defines herself as someone living life as fully as she can, which for her means to be involved in a relationship, bearing a child, without a husband, and even without Fred, if need be. Her courage and example, her love and devotion convert Frederic Henry from a selfish, uncaring individual to one who loves, who shares, and who serves others. Since this is a first-person narrative told by Frederic Henry, one cannot see how this lesson lasts after Catherine's death, except in the act of narration itself, a tribute to her memory. One can see, though, Henry's and Hemingway's revulsion with war:

I had seen nothing sacred, and the things that were glorious had no glory and the sacrifices were like the stockyards at Chicago if nothing was done with the meat except to bury it. ... Abstract words such as glory, honor, courage, or hallow were obscene beside the concrete names of villages, the numbers of roads, the names of rivers, the numbers of regiments, and the dates. (p. 185)

Although the serialization of the novel in *Scribner's Magazine* was banned in Boston (after all, Frederic and Catherine were not married, and not terribly anxious to be so), the novel was successful, selling twenty-eight thousand copies in a month in the fall of 1929, before the stock market crashed. Hemingway's simple prose and plots of love and violence allowed him to write what he and literary critics could take as literature, but which the common reader could take as good entertainment. As such, Hemingway's novels were more commercially successful than those of F. Scott Fitzgerald (after his first) and of William Faulkner. But the Depression was not a financially lucrative time for most serious novelists.

Hemingway's next book, *Death in the Afternoon* (1932) aroused the ire of critics for a number of reasons. First, it was a serious, nonfiction study of bullfighting, a subject not close to the hearts of most American critics. Second, as I have already said, the subject seemed irrelevant in the social and economic turmoil of the Depression. And third, even for those critics who deigned to give it a serious reading, Hemingway's constant praise of physical courage seemed further evidence of his narrow, macho views, juvenile romanticism, and unsophisticated philosophy.

Death in the Afternoon is several books masquerading as one. It is a serious, scholarly (487-page) study of bullfighting, complete with 96 pages of captioned photographs (selected by Hemingway), a glossary of technical terms, a schedule of Spanish bullfighting dates, an assessment of American matador Sidney Franklin, detailed reactions to bullfighting by several of Hemingway's acquaintances, and a bibliographical note, including this explanation: *Death in the Afternoon* "is intended as an introduction to the modern Spanish bullfight and attempts to explain that spectacle both emotionally and practically" (p. 487). But the tome is also more: it includes travelogue, autobiography, capsule biographies of then-current bullfighters with critical analyses of their styles, and philosophical discussions about death in Iberian and Anglo cultures, and about aesthetics. It is a modern omnium-gatherum, like the great Renaissance essay collections using a single topic as a focus by Robert Burton or Sir Thomas Browne. It can be argued that by combining all these Hemingway slighted all but bullfighting; certainly he confused his reviewers, who should have seen that in writing about the combination of artfully styled violent death, he was indirectly describing his own approach to his usual subject matter.

At the beginning of the book, he writes the passage I quoted in chapter 2 about "knowing truly what you really felt" and capturing "the sequence of motion and fact which made the emotion that you experienced" (p. 2). He goes on to say,

The only place where you could see life and death, *i.e.*, violent death now that the wars were over, was in the bull ring and I wanted very much to go to Spain where I could study it. I was trying to learn to write, commencing with the simplest things, and one of the simplest things of all and the most fundamental is violent death. (p. 2)

Thus, Hemingway announces the thematic thread of mortality and how we deal with it early on; it was obviously a personal problem, one forcefully encountered at war and returned to from such early stories as *In Our Time* interchapters 2, 3, 5, 7, to "Indian Camp" and beyond. And it was a problem familiar to the Spanish people of Castille.

They know death is the unescapable reality, the one thing any man may be sure of. . . . They take an intelligent interest in death and when they can see it given, avoided, refused and accepted in the afternoon for a nominal price of admission they pay their money and go to the bull ring. (p. 266)

As I explained in discussing *The Sun Also Rises*, Hemingway believed that the spectator shares with the bullfighter the emotion of forestalling death. For the price of admission, temporarily, the witness is godlike and immortal. "The essence of the greatest emotional appeal of bullfighting is the feeling of immortality that the bullfighter . . . gives to the spectators" (*Death in the Afternoon*, p. 213). Thus Hemingway excuses bullfighting, and hunting, saying,

Killing cleanly and in a way which gives you aesthetic pleasure and pride has always been one of the greatest enjoyments of a part of the human race. . . . When a man is still in rebellion against death he has pleasure in taking to himself one of the God-like attributes; that of giving it. (pp. 232–33)

Over and above what Hemingway is saying about bullfighters, he seems to say that as hunter and soldier he enjoys playing God, taking life as a show of force before his own can be taken; it is a statement he will make again in *Green Hills of Africa*.

The short story "The Natural History of the Dead," which appears in *Death in the Afternoon*, can then be interpreted as a garrulous digression, a piece of padding in an already-long book, or, more properly, it should be seen as a thematic excursion on a major subject of the book, as the other stories and aesthetic discussion should also be seen as thematically relevant excursions, even if they are not announced with chapter headings and authorial explanations.

Hemingway was moved to write *Death in the Afternoon*, not only because of his own interest in bullfighting, but because he felt that the sport/art was in decline, a period of decadence as he repeatedly calls it, and so he wrote to describe, historically, what had been, how the sport had developed, and how it was, including suggestions for its emendation and restoration. (He acknowledges, however, that the newspapers of each generation lament the falling off from an earlier golden era, a period whose journals also lament a falling off from before.) For the modern American reader, there are undoubtedly too many lists of bullfighters, banderilleros, breeding ranches, etc. For any but the most dedicated aficionados (lovers of bullfighting), Hemingway's discriminations between the various bullfighters of the late twenties, early thirties, although they contribute to his aesthetic discussions, probably hold less interest than would discussions evaluating the catching or hitting ability of minor league baseball players of the same era.

At times, the prose lacks his concentrated compactness. At other times, it imitates marvelously the action it describes:

The bull turned very quickly and Gitanillo turned with the muleta ["heart-shaped scarlet cloth ... doubled over a tapered
wooden stick" (p. 423)] to let him come by on the left, raised the
muleta and then rose himself in the air, his legs widespread, his
hands still holding the muleta, his head down, the bull's left horn
in his thigh. The bull turned him on the horn and threw him
against the barrera. The bull's horn found him, picked him up
once more and threw him against the wood again. Then as he lay
there the bull drove the horn through his back. (p. 218)

In other, less-bloody passages, Hemingway poetically re-
creates scenes and smells that are for him the essence of
Spain:

If I could ... make clouds coming fast in shadows moving over
wheat and the small, careful stepping horses; the smell of olive
oil; the feel of leather; rope soled shoes; the loops of twisted gar-
lics; earthen pots; saddle bags carried across the shoulder; wine
skins; the pitchforks made of natural wood (the tines were
branches); the early morning smells; the cold mountain nights
and the long hot days of summer, with always trees and shade
under the trees, then you would have a little of Navarra. But it's
not in this book. (p. 275)

But, of course, it is in the book; you have just read it. You
must supply your own "early morning smells," your own
"cold mountain nights" and "long hot days of summer,"
but Hemingway convinces you that you do now know
something of Spain, as you now know a good deal about
bullfighting. Like Hemingway's characters, you have been
initiated; whether you have acquired true aficionado is another matter.

Hemingway's introduction to the book with his own
comments about the craft of writing tie in to his discussion
of the decadence of bullfighting and his criticisms of matadors. In *The Sun Also Rises* he had written about Romero's
giving true emotion because his style was "straight and
pure and natural in line" (p. 168), a sentence I claimed that
Hemingway was using self-reflexively. In *Death in the Afternoon*, he repeatedly criticizes bullfighters who trick, who

cheat, who stab the bull without exposing themselves to danger ("assassins," Hemingway calls them). A true artist of the ring will move his spectators. The final third of a bullfight

takes a man out of himself and makes him feel immortal while it is proceeding [and] gives him an ecstasy, that is, while momentary, as profound as any religious ecstasy; . . . a growing ecstasy of ordered, passionate, increasing disregard for death that leaves you, when it is over, . . . as empty, as changed and as sad as any major emotion will leave you. (pp. 206–7)

As Frost would say, "The figure is the same as for love."[4] Beyond bullfighting and sexual passion, both writers are talking about the possibilities of great art. Hemingway is making a parallel between artists, whether matadors or writers, who risk greatly, expose themselves, in order to confer great emotion and momentary feelings of immortality, who hold death off for a moment with their art. Anything less is trickery and shameful. And, although he never makes the claim, it is obvious that he considers himself among the true artists, rather than a cheating entertainer.

Altogether, though, the nonfiction format of *Death in the Afternoon* is slower, less exciting than his fiction had been, for the most part, up until that time. The bullfighters and their flaws have aesthetic significance, but the lists of bullfighters, their banderilleros, and all the rest of the minutiae of bullfighting detail that Hemingway includes is of little interest to most readers. Earlier he had picked universal events with which one could identify, and he picked objects in context that did in fact seem to convey the emotion he wanted conveyed. In *Death in the Afternoon,* his choices were often more personal, less universal, thus less accessible for most readers.

His next collection of short stories, *Winner Take Nothing* (1933), titled for his philosophical belief that loss was inevitable, that no victory could be sustained, is disappointing. Only one story is truly exceptional, "A Clean, Well-Lighted Place," a study of existential despair.[5] An aged man, nearly

deaf, has had a suicide attempt interrupted by his niece.
Now he waits for death, in one form or another, and drinks
in the evenings at a café, clean, well-lighted, orderly, an oasis in the sea of despair, an island of comfort in an ocean of
no reasons for living. He is presented to us through the dialogue of two waiters, one young and still confident, sure
of himself and his place in life, one older, who shares the
old man's despair.

"You have youth, confidence, and a job," the older waiter said.
"You have everything."
"And what do you lack?"
"Everything but work."
"You have everything I have."
"No. I have never had confidence and I am not young."
(*Short Stories*, p. 382)

Again, Hemingway forces the reader to pay close attention
to who is talking. (In fact, there is a critical controversy insisting that two lines were mixed up in the printing and
spacially assigned to the wrong waiters.) Again, the scene
and the words of those involved carry all meaning.

After he has closed the café, the older waiter seeks an
oasis for himself so that he can avoid going to an empty
abode and painful, thought-wracked sleeplessness.

What did he fear? It was not fear or dread. It was a nothing that
he knew too well. It was all a nothing and a man was nothing
too. It was only that and light was needed and a certain cleanness
and order. Some lived in it and never felt it, but he knew it was
all nada [nothing] y pues [and then] nada y nada y pues nada.
Our nada who art in nada, nada be they name thy kingdom nada
thy will be nada in nada as it is in nada.   (p. 383)

Hemingway makes the absence of an extrinsic code of values based on sure knowledge of divine existence into a pal-
pable force, a monstrous nothing of despair. People are
nothing and existence is nothing, except for what people
make out of their lives by their actions: existentialism. And
his blasphemous parody of "The Lord's Prayer" accentuates
his point.

Stories such as "A Sea Change" and "The Mother of a Queen" deal with homosexuality, a topic that Hemingway dealt with in *Death in the Afternoon* and will deal with at much greater length in *The Garden of Eden*, but the despair of "A Clean, Well-Lighted Place" infects most of the stories in *Winner Take Nothing*, making it a depressing volume, largely unrelieved by the courage of a Jake, a Manuel Garcia, or a Catherine. The final story in the volume, "Fathers and Sons" (title from Turgenev), shows Nick Adams as father, talking to his son, remembering his father, Doctor Adams of the earlier stories, and his own sexual initiation. Hemingway strings together a series of adverbs to try to create in prose the rhythm and building tension and release of sexual intercourse, as he will do again in *For Whom the Bell Tolls*. Nick alludes indirectly to his father's suicide, as Robert Jordan will refer explicitly to his father's suicide in *For Whom the Bell Tolls*, and he alludes to himself as writer and his attempts to come to terms with experience by writing about it; here again, there is a parallel to the bullfighter, an artistic shaping of experience. "Fathers and Sons" is a nostalgic story, both in content and tone, as Nick strives for greater closeness with his son than his father had achieved with him, and it closes the volume with an elegiac tone. But Nick is as reticent discussing sexual matters as his father had been, and biographically the occasion of the story is Hemingway's driving his eldest son to Arkansas to meet his stepmother and stepbrothers; thus we have to wonder whether Nick can achieve great closeness with his son, or whether the author is showing the impossibility of bridging the generational gap, the inevitable chasm between fathers and sons.

The quasi-autobiographical nature of "Fathers and Sons" becomes distinct autobiography in Hemingway's next book, *The Green Hills of Africa* (1935), an account of a safari he and Pauline had taken, accompanied by a Key West friend Charles Thompson, in Kenya and Tanzania in late 1933, early 1934. The book is ostensibly nonfiction, although as critics and even historians now say any record of events is only one version of them. Fiction and nonfiction are on a continuum. The fictional *The Sun Also Rises* is based on real people, with their names changed, and real events; *The Green Hills of Africa* is based on real events, but only half of the characters have their names changed: Hemingway keeps his, as does the native M'Cola, and the natives nicknamed Garrick and Droopy; the white hunter Philip Percival becomes Pop or Mr. Jackson Phillips, Charles Thompson becomes Karl, Ben Fourie becomes Dan, and Hans Koritschoner becomes Kandinsky. Hemingway's foreword insists, as I've quoted, that "the writer has attempted to write an absolutely true book to see whether . . . [it can] compete with a work of the imagination." For most of the contemporary critics and reviewers, it could not, and I agree with them.

The left-wing reviewers were again annoyed, as they had been by *Death in the Afternoon,* by the irrelevancy of big-game hunting during the economic hardships of the Depression, by Hemingway's lack of social concern. Others were disturbed by a prose no longer as taut and compelling as it had once been. Hemingway was changing his prose style slightly, experimenting with more than just the form of the book. Unlike a journal narrative, *The Green Hills of Africa* begins in medias res, then, after three chapters, has a seven-chapter flashback, and ends before the safari does with a brief conclusion in Israel at the Sea of Galilee. The artistic arrangement of the material, the discussion of literature and writers at the book's opening, and the change of Kortischoner's name to that of the Russian abstract expressionist painter, Wassily Kandinsky, all suggest that, like *Death in the Afternoon, The Green Hills of Africa* is also about art.

In his conversation with the character Kandinsky, almost an interview, the character Hemingway discusses his dislike for Ralph Waldo Emerson, Nathaniel Hawthorne, and John Whittier, his inability to read Henry Thoreau, and his delight in Mark Twain: "All modern American literature comes from one book by Mark Twain called *Huckleberry Finn*" (p. 22). He also discusses the economic and critical pitfalls that beset an American writer. When Kandinsky, like the American critics, denounces Hemingway's hunting as juvenile and unworthy of a man of his literary gifts, Hemingway insists that a writer needs experiences to write about, and that hunting is both something he enjoys and a source of interesting material. He enjoys hunting for reasons discussed in *Death in the Afternoon,* as an exercise in power, as quoted before:

Killing cleanly and in a way which gives you aesthetic pleasure and pride has always been one of the greatest enjoyments of a part of the human race.... (*Death in the Afternoon* p. 232)

And while I can understand intellectually what Hemingway means by "aesthetic pleasure," and I can certainly understand the moral obligation once one decides to hunt of shooting an animal accurately in a vital spot so that it suffers little, like many of his critics, I still have difficulty with the concept of aesthetic killing, which to me is an oxymoron. I know that Hemingway is likening hunting to bullfighting and to writing, that he is saying that there is a right and proper, a skillful way to do all things, and I would agree, but I find the analogy here stretched considerably. Hemingway continues his justification, saying:

I did nothing that had not been done to me. I had been shot and I had been crippled and gotten away. I expected, always, to be killed by one thing or another and I, truly, did not mind that any more. Since I still loved to hunt I resolved that I would shoot as long as I could kill cleanly and as soon as I lost that ability I would stop. (*The Green Hills of Africa* p. 148)

I did not mind killing anything, any animal, if I killed it cleanly, they all had to die and my interference with the nightly and the seasonal killing that went on all the time was very minute and I had no guilty feeling at all. (*The Green Hills of Africa* p. 272)

This last passage occurs after he has mistakenly killed a sable cow and then twice shot and wounded a sable bull without being able to kill it. Although he protests "we ate the meat and kept the hides and horns," a few years later in

Cuba he shot hundreds of live pigeons as target practice, and on a jackrabbit hunt in Idaho, his younger sons "killed eighty each, and Ernest and Martha swelled the total to almost four hundred."[6] Thus, it is obvious that *The Green Hills of Africa*, like *Death in the Afternoon* before it, is a meditation on death. Whatever may be fictional in the presentation and arrangement, the grappling with death and the attempt to control it is surely nonfiction.

If Hemingway did not change his subject matter to suit the critics, he was willing to experiment with changes in style. Sentences grew in length. On pages 5–6, there is a 163-word sentence; on pages 70–71, one of 253 words, involving both stream of consciousness and an explicitly poetic style:

how fine the fountains were at the Place de L'Observatoire (*water sheen rippling on the bronze of horses' manes, bronze breasts and shoulders, green under thin-flowing water*) and when they put up the bust of Flaubert in the Luxembourg on the short cut through the gardens on the way to rue Soufflot (*one that we believed in, loved without criticism, heavy now in stone as an idol should be*).

The influence of Joyce is obvious here (perhaps refracted, more closely, through Faulkner). But these longer sentences (one extends from page 148 to page 150) and the poetic passages are experiments that are not integral with the rest of Hemingway's book, and instead of making his prose seem new, the author just seems garrulous. He is condescending to Pauline, addressed as P.O.M. throughout (Poor Old Mother), whose primary concern is whether her fancy boots fit, condescending to the natives, and even to fellow hunter Karl. Passages of action are described with excitement, with the "sequence of motion and fact which made the emotion," but much of the book is reflective and even vapid:

in my grandfather's time, Michigan was a malaria ridden state. They called it fever and ague. And in the Tortugas, where I'd spent months, a thousand men once died of yellow fever. New continents and islands try to frighten you with disease as a snake hisses. The snake may be poisonous too. You kill them off. Hell, what I had a month ago [dysentery] would have killed me in the old days before they invented the remedies. Maybe it would and maybe I would have gotten well. (p. 284)

The same page continues with some interesting conservationist observations:

A continent ages quickly once we come. The natives live in harmony with it. But the foreigner destroys, cuts down the trees, drains the water, so that the water supply is altered, and in a short time the soil, once the sod is turned under, is cropped out and . . . starts to blow away.

He concludes this lecture by saying, "Let the others come to America who did not know that they had come too late. Our people had seen it at its best and fought for it when it was well worth fighting for. Now I would go somewhere else" (p. 285).

The conclusion of the book at the Sea of Galilee is an attempt to suggest that the book, "nonfictional" account of an actual hunt though it be, is really an attempt to achieve something not merely temporal and evanescent, but a permanent achievement. Hemingway told Kandinsky that he was striving for

the kind of writing that can be done. How far prose can be carried if any one is serious enough and has luck. There is a fourth and fifth dimension that can be gotten. . . . It is much more difficult than poetry. . . . But it can be written, without tricks and without cheating. With nothing that will go bad afterwards. (pp. 26–27)

A country, finally, erodes and the dust blows away, the people all die and none of them were of any importance permanently, except those that practised the arts. . . . A thousand years makes economics silly and a work of art endures forever. (p. 109)

More condescension to unimportant people (even to those who discovered the treatment for his dysentery), but an implicit claim for the importance of art and for *The Green*

Hills of Africa as art of that magnitude. It *will* last and be read because Hemingway wrote it, but I, at least, find no fourth and fifth dimension within it, and little permanent and imperishable art.

4

Depressing Times

Hemingway's next book, the novel *To Have and Have Not* (1937), is even worse, although it went through four printings in two months. There is little within it worth quoting, except to contrast unfavorably with his writing at its best. The book began as two short stories, part 1 published in *Cosmopolitan* in 1934 as "One Trip Across," part 2 in *Esquire* in 1936 as "The Tradesman's Return." Hemingway added a long third section (171 pages) to the 87 pages of the first two parts, but the three never make a cohesive novel, in spite of the presence of Harry Morgan throughout.

Hemingway was moved by the plight of homeless World War I veterans who, sixteen years after the war, were without benefits and were working for the government for six and seven dollars a week doing construction work. At the end of the summer in 1935, they were struck by a hurricane with no warning and without having any adequate shelter; nearly a thousand drowned. Hemingway was furious and denounced the government's lack of concern in an article for *The New Masses*. This concern carries over into the novel, whose title indicates that Hemingway was paying at least lip service to the social concerns of the Depression decade, the gap between rich and poor. But the novel is not convincing as an economic study, nor is it convincing as a depiction of a hero exemplifying an admirable code of conduct, a study of the poor, a satire of the rich, or a criticism of the ineptitude of government.

At the start of the novel, Harry Morgan is chartering his thirty-eight-foot boat (same length as the *Pilar*) for fishing cruises and has brought a customer from Key West to Cuba. The opening scene describes three Cuban revolutionaries asking to be smuggled off the island, Harry refusing them, and then the three being gunned down in front of the café, as Harry watches from the shelter of the bar, impassively, not even telling the reader who the "we" in his narration refers to or what happens to the other person for five pages. The shooting sets the tone of violence for the novel and establishes Harry (pirate-named as he is) as a cool, tough individual. His fisherman-customer takes the plane back to the States, ducking out on Harry and his $825 debt for chartering the boat and losing expensive tackle by not following Harry's directions, leaving Harry in Cuba without enough money to buy gas to get back to Key West, and without necessary fishing tackle for the future. Harry thus agrees to pick up Chinese who wish to go to the States, but Mr. Sing, who makes the arrangements, wants Harry to kill his passengers, not transport them. Rather than kill twelve people, Harry takes Mr. Sing's money and kills him, strangling him with his bare hands, a strange application of Benthamite utilitarianism, and then lands the twelve Chinese back on Cuba.

The following fall, his money gone—Harry has a wife and three daughters to support, and he's bought a second engine for his boat—he takes to smuggling rum from Cuba, and he and his deckhand are shot leaving Cuba, Wesley in the leg, Harry in the right arm, the bullet shattering the upper arm (as Hemingway's upper right arm was broken in his car accident in Wyoming). Even though wounded, Harry steers the boat across to the Keys, and is dumping the liquor overboard, by himself, one-handedly, when two vacationing government officials see him and report him as a smuggler. Harry loses both his arm and his boat.

In the long third part, Hemingway counterpoints Harry's attempts to take four Cuban revolutionaries and bank robbers from Key West to Cuba, and the shootings that ensue, with life at Key West: accounts of a radical novelist, Richard Gordon, punch-drunk veterans drinking their pay for government relief work in a local bar, and the decadent rich

on their yachts. The criticism of the rich has not been well
prepared for and is not integral to the novel, the title notwithstanding. Similarly, the contrast between Harry's pre-
sumed craftmanship as fisherman, sailor, and killer and the
poor fictional art of Richard Gordon, insufficiently based
on personal experience and true understanding, is less apparent and less convincing than the parallels between art
and life in either *Death in the Afternoon* or *The Green
Hills of Africa.*

The faults of the novel, besides lack of integration of
parts, are numerous. Hemingway has exemplified code heroes, men good at their trade but at little else, in characters
like Jack Brennan of "Fifty Grand" and in Wilson of "The
Short Happy Life of Francis Macomber." Brennan is stingy,
anti-Semitic, and mean-tempered, but he was an excellent
boxer and he is willing to take great physical punishment to
support his wife and children. Hemingway asks us to admire his quick-wittedness, his endurance, and his commitment to his craft, not all his behavior. And he may have
intended the same with Harry Morgan, but there's little to
like about Morgan. Neither he nor his wife likes their children. Harry may be good in bed, but that's not much of a
recommendation for the general reader. A friend describes
him as a bully (p. 99), as does a business associate not a
friend (p. 122). Harry is cruel, selfish, and a racist: " 'Hell,'
said Harry, 'ain't no nigger any good when he's shot.
You're a all right nigger, Wesley' " (p. 87). And he is entirely willing to shoot a friend to eliminate a witness to his
murder of Sing (pp. 60, 63). There's nothing to recommend
him except his competence, almost nothing to engage the
reader. What's worse, Harry owns his thirty-eight-foot boat
with dual engines, a house with a piano, and a car. He has
been a policeman in Miami, is a skilled fisherman and qual-
ified boat captain. Hemingway simply does not convince
us, bad as the Depression was, that Harry has to turn to
smuggling and murder to support himself and his family.

Disturbing also is the sense that some of Harry's failings
are those of the author—especially the racism. While the
bigotry quoted above is in Harry's speech, some comes

from the third-person narrator: the use of "nigger" throughout most of the novel, the implication that a white man better endures a more serious wound than a black does, not only enduring the wound but performing needed tasks while wounded (pp. 70, 75), and the description of shops as "Jew stores" (p. 193).

That Hemingway depicts a measure of altruism, labeled as brotherhood, does not convince the reader of great social solidarity among the Key West proletariat. For example, Harry thanks Captain Willie for warning him that the vacationing government men have seen him dumping liquor overboard, saying "Thanks, brother." When the government men ask Willie if Harry is indeed his brother, Willie replies that "Most everybody goes in boats calls each other brother" (p. 83). Again, later in the novel, Richard Gordon's marriage breaks up, and the man to whom Gordon's wife turns is sorry for Gordon, especially after Gordon tries to drink himself into oblivion. He loads the drunken Gordon into a taxi, in spite of Gordon's efforts to hit him, telling the questioning cab driver that Gordon is, in a way, his brother (p. 221). We are all our brothers' keepers. But Harry Morgan's last words—"No matter how a man alone ain't got a bloody fucking chance" (p. 225)—while they prepare the reader for the concept of social solidarity that *For Whom the Bell Tolls*'s "No man is an island" will express, simply are not adequately prepared for or convincing. The focus of the novel is on Harry's toughness, and while he fails, Hemingway does not convince the reader that it was from lack of help from others, any more than he has convinced us that economic hard times alone made Harry a criminal.

In places, the dialogue is simply inept. Marie, Harry's wife, helps him fuel his boat and tells him how much she cares for him:

"You know I lay awake almost four hours just thinking about you."
"You're some old woman."
"I can think about you any time and get excited."
"Well, we got to fill this gas now," Harry told her.   (p. 117)

Or Richard Gordon's wife, in part of his diatribe against her husband, says, "You wouldn't marry me in the church and it broke my poor mother's heart as you well know" (p. 185). Sometimes, the prose is torturous and unclear:

If he had not been felt to be cracking up, with that instinct for feeling something wrong with a member of the pack and healthy desire to turn him out, if it is impossible to destroy him which characterizes the rich; he would not have been reduced to accepting the hospitality of Wallace Johnson. (p. 232)

Hemingway juxtaposes the struggling poor against the decadent rich. These latter include a homosexual (Wallace Johnson, above), a suicidal bisexual, a voyeuristic husband observing his promiscuous wife in bed with other men, an impotent tax fraud who has ruined and driven many to suicide, and the masturbating wife of a cirrhotic Hollywood director whose lover has not satisfied her. These sexually troubled individuals are provided by the author as contrasts to the satisfying sex life of Harry and Marie; Hemingway suggests that the money leads to abnormal, and by 1930s' standards, perverse sexuality. But he doesn't arouse the reader's compassion for the poor because he does not show their daily life, the heroism of their struggles, or their compassion and humanity as superior to that of the rich, focusing as he does on the adventures of Harry Morgan. And when the reader should feel grief and sympathy for the poor, Hemingway undercuts it. The Cuban bank robbers, before shooting Harry, shoot Albert Tracy, his deckhand. When Harry's boat is towed in, Albert's wife is at the dock, grieving, and is described by Hemingway as "gaunt, middle-aged and bare-headed, and her stringy hair had come undone and was down on her neck although it was still knotted at the end." Pushed off the dock by crowding spectators, who do nothing to save her, she is finally rescued by two Coast Guard Sailors.

As she stood dripping on the stern, she looked up at [the crowd] . . . and shouted, "Basards! Bishes!"
. . . "My plate," said Mrs. Tracy tragically. "Losht my plate." (pp. 250–53)

Hemingway makes the spectators, who are as poor as Mrs.
Tracy, into an unsympathetic mob, and he undercuts her
grief with slapstick comedy, destroying any effective contrast between rich and poor.

He continued experimenting with his prose, telling Part
One in first person, Part Two in third person, using both in
Part Three and several narrators, but the varying points of
view add little. Harry is made to say such stupid things as:

> You know how it is there early in the morning in Havana with
> the bums still asleep against the walls of the buildings.   (p. 3)

> You know how you feel when you hit a drunk.   (p. 38)

And critics like Philip Young have responded, "No. How
does it feel to hit a drunk? Tell us how it feels to hit a
drunk."[1] In his *Paris Review* interview with George
Plimpton, Hemingway said, "The most essential gift for a
good writer is a built-in, shock-proof, shit detector."[2] In
writing *To Have and Have Not,* his own sensitive ear, his
own detector, failed him.

Hemingway's next book-length publication was the com-
pendium *The Fifth Column and the First Forty-Nine
Stories,* published in October of 1938. It contains Hemingway's only full-scale play (as well as the one-acter, "Today
Is Friday," about Christ's crucifixion, originally published
in *Men Without Women*) and Hemingway's collected stories
up to that point.[3] The play, *The Fifth Column,* is about a
fictional Hemingway alter ego—"with the big shoulders
and the walk like a gorilla and the funny face" (p. 58)—
who masquerades as a war correspondent during the Spanish Civil War while actually engaging in counterespionage
activities, a strange variation on the mild-mannered re-
porter/superhero syndrome.

Rawlings rarely submits stories to the censorship office,
and is often drunk. Dorothy Bridges, with whom he falls in
love, accuses him of being a playboy, yet there must have
been more fashionable watering holes between 1936–39
than Madrid, without fresh food and constantly under enemy fire. What do the other correspondents and civilians

think when Rawlings is frequently escorted by an armed guard? That aspect of the plot is thin to transparency. Rawlings drinks to forget the dirtiness of his job, the torture of those captured for information and the killing, not in the heat of combat or at long range, but close up and messy. He wants a life, not under fire and the threat of death, and a relationship with a woman, rather than the ministrations of local whores, and Dorothy Bridges seems to him ideal for that end.

She is a fellow correspondent, Vassar-educated, though one who doesn't understand what is happening militarily. She is beautiful, tall, and blonde. She is also stupid, not only in not understanding the war she is covering, but in not knowing why her lover leaves her bed many evenings, is constantly called on the phone or calling, barking orders, sometimes in code, carries a pistol, and is accompanied by guards. As far as Dorothy can see, his whole life is a waste of time. She is delighted when Rawlings beats up another correspondent who has the room adjoining Dorothy's and has been sharing her bed, and moves in instead. She finds Philip much more attractive than her married lover; Philip's "so lovely and so sort of *vital* and so gay. But he doesn't *do* anything" (p. 25). While the Madrilenos are starving, Dorothy eats tinned *civet lièvre* (jugged hare), *foie gras* (pâté), and *poulet de Bresse* (chicken from Bresse, an area in France famous for its poultry) brought in to Madrid from Paris in diplomatic pouches. She also takes advantage of the war-caused inflation and an advantageous exchange rate to buy a silver fox cape. Hemingway uses her as a symbol for all those who know of the war but don't care, don't help, don't do. While that criticism of rich, smug, isolationist Americans is understandable, it is less credible that Philip Rawlings would fall passionately in love with someone so unconcerned with the deaths around her, given his own dedication to the Loyalist, Republican cause.

Thus, at the play's end, when Philip feels that he must choose between the warm arms and bed of Dorothy Bridges and his commitment to fight, undistracted, so that "men will not have to fear ill health or old age; so that they can

live and work in dignity and not as slaves," his choice,
while poignant, hardly seems tragic. Dorothy, physically attractive though she is, hardly seems a suitable mate for a
clandestine hero, a Zorro or Scarlet Pimpernel. Besides,
Philip has the fiery Moorish tart Anita, eager to console
him for giving up Dorothy.

In addition to the characters already named, there are
Philip's hard-bitten commander, who is a direct descendant
of medieval Spanish inquisitors, and a German spy named
Max whom the Fascists have tortured: "A comrade with his
teeth gone in front? With sort of black gums where they
burnt them with a red hot iron? And with a scar here? *He
runs his fingers across the lower angle of his jaw*" (p. 44).
There is also the hotel manager, whose imperfect English
results in comic malapropisms: "You take away the young
lady. Make him *furious*. Fills him with, how you call it,
jellishness."

Over all, the play is talky, the only extended scene of action being a raid on a Fascist artillery observation post,
manned by both Spaniards and Germans. And the drum
rolls for cannonading, the splintered glass, while exciting,
hardly give any more true sense of the horror of war than
does the hotel manager's constant begging for tins of food,
comically undercut as his requests are by his faulty English.
The reader sees Philip engaged in a cause, not well explained, certainly not fifty years after the events, desiring a
private life and unable to have one, but doesn't know him
well enough to care. It's not a bad play, but it's not a very
good one.

Three stories in *The First Forty-Nine* deserve mention.
The first, "Up in Michigan," was written in 1921 and first
printed in Paris in *Three Stories and Ten Poems* in 1923;
neither Boni & Liveright nor Scribner's reprinted it in the
intervening years because of its overt sexuality (including
the sexual pun on an erection in the title). It is a story by a
young Hemingway, still shaping his style, and the repetitions, the influence of Gertrude Stein, are obvious and at
times excessive (see the passage quoted below). The story
concerns the defloration of a naive young girl working in a

rooming house in Hortons Bay, Michigan (Hemingway gave his characters the names of real people whom he knew at Horton Bay, Michigan, causing much consternation among them and in his family).

The girl, Liz, is attracted to a blacksmith, Jim Gilmore, and the story is her initiation into an unromantic world. Liz does not understand her feelings, and has no one to talk to about them: is it love or merely a first infatuation?

> Liz liked Jim very much. She liked it the way he walked over from the shop and often went to the kitchen door to watch for him down the road. She liked it about his mustache. She liked it about how white his teeth were when he smiled. She liked it very much that he didn't look like a blacksmith. (p. 81)

Gilmore "liked her face because it was so jolly but he never thought about her" (p. 81). He spears fish in an unsportsmanlike manner by jacklight; and when he returns from a hunting trip he makes with others, of the three deer they have killed only one is identified as a buck, the implication being that two does have also been killed. Gilmore is a hunter concerned with results, not the law, niceties, or others' feelings. One night, well liquored, he takes advantage of Liz's inchoate romantic yearnings and seduces her, forcing himself upon her.

> The hemlock planks of the dock were hard and splintery and cold and Jim was heavy on her and he had hurt her. Liz pushed him, she was so uncomfortable and cramped. Jim was asleep.... She worked out from under him.... Jim was sleeping with his mouth a little open. Liz leaned over and kissed him on the cheek. He was still asleep.... She was cold and miserable and everything felt gone.
> ... Liz took off her coat and leaned over and covered him with it.... Then she walked across the dock and up the steep sandy road to go to bed. A cold mist was coming up through the woods from the bay. (pp. 85–86)

There the story ends, with the cold mist of reality blotting out the warm, romantic dreams of a young girl. She is cruelly initiated, comparable to the lessons learned by Nick

Adams in stories that Hemingway was then writing for *In Our Time;* in the common vernacular, both of them are screwed over. And in spite of the story's harsh reality, in this story, as in "Hills Like White Elephants," Hemingway's sympathies are clearly with the female character.

"The Short Happy Life of Francis Macomber" and "The Snows of Kilimanjaro" are stories based on Hemingway's African safari earlier in the decade.[4] Both deal with initiation, an epiphany of self-awareness that occurs close to the story protagonist's death, and both continue the experiments in prose style begun with *The Green Hills of Africa.* "Macomber" is about a thirty-five-year-old, rich American on safari with his lovely wife. It opens in medias res, with the Macombers at lunch after Francis, with his wife as witness, had bolted in cowardice from a wounded lion, leaving the white hunter Wilson to kill it. The story is told by the narrator in omniscient third person, giving us the scene and the point of view predominantly of the two men, but sometimes the thoughts of Francis's wife Margot, and sometimes even those of the lion.

After telling us that Macomber has fled from the wounded lion, Hemingway then flashes back and gives us Francis's fear, waking in the night and hearing the lion roar, his trepidation before the hunt, his inability to confess his fright or discuss it with anyone, and his fear during the hunt itself. Although Hemingway doesn't develop the topic at length, he does look here at the conventional macho code of courage he has long measured his characters by, the code of bravado and gun-in-hand courage that critics had long criticized.

The Macombers' marriage is not a happy one, but "Margot was too beautiful for Macomber to divorce her and Macomber had too much money for Margot ever to leave him." In disgust with her husband's cowardice, Margot cuckolds him with Wilson, the narrator implying that it is not her first infidelity. The next morning, Macomber, aware of the infidelity, is furious, and takes his anger out on the buffalo they are shooting, without any preliminary fears of

them to distract him. Again, Hemingway's prose marvelously captures the sense of ongoing action, his increasingly
long sentences put to good effect:

and then, the car swaying as though it had just jumped a road,
they drew up close and he could see the plunging hugeness of the
bull, . . . and he was raising his rifle when Wilson shouted, "Not
from the car, you fool!" and he had no fear, only hatred of Wilson, while the brakes clamped on and the car skidded, plowing
sideways to an almost stop and Wilson was out on one side and
he was on the other, stumbling as his feet hit the still speeding-by
of the earth, and then he was shooting at the bull as he moved
away, hearing the bullets whunk into him, emptying his rifle at
him as he moved steadily away. (pp. 27–28)

One buffalo is not killed, and as Macomber and Wilson
go into the brush to finish it off, it charges them, as the lion
had the day before, but now Francis stands his ground to
fire at it, a new man, no longer afraid of animals, of death,
or of his wife. Wilson muses: "he had seen men come of
age before. . . . It was not a matter of their twenty-first
birthday. . . . More of a change than any loss of virginity.
Fear gone like an operation. . . . Made him into a man.
Women knew it too. No bloody fear" (pp. 32–33). This
sudden access of manhood is Macomber's "happy life," and
it is short indeed. As the buffalo charges at him, Margot,
witnessing the scene from the car, directly in back of him,
shoots at the buffalo and hits her husband, killing him.

There has been much critical debate as to whether Margot, aware that she will no longer dominate her husband,
intentionally shoots him, accidentally shoots him, or, in a
Freudian slip, accidentally shoots him on purpose. The text
says that she "shot at the buffalo" (p. 36), and she has only
a split second to pick up her rifle and shoot; nor has the
story established her as someone capable of placing her
shots with great accuracy under that duress, especially
when seasoned hunters like her husband and Wilson are
also missing their shots. An accident seems most likely. But
the point of the story is not her intentions when she fires.

"The Short Happy Life" is a story about, again, the inevitability of losing and of doing so with dignity: Francis was standing his ground against the buffalo and against his own fears when he was killed. But it is also a story, like *The Sun Also Rises*, about control, self-control, and control of others. Initially, Francis can control neither his wife nor his own fear; Margot dominates him. Mastering his fear, he gains ascendancy over her. She, learning that it is illegal to pursue game in cars, gains a weapon over Wilson, one that would remove his license, drive him out of business. Wilson then uses Margot's shooting her husband to regain his own position of dominance: Margot needs his testimony to establish that the shooting was an accident. As these individuals seek to assert their power over animals, so they do against each other. Hemingway has used a hunting story, its events and tensions, to describe the human animal and its behavior.

The other African story in the collection, "Snows of Kilimanjaro," also concerns a death, this time of a writer named Harry. Harry and his rich wife, at least his second, have been on safari, and Harry has improperly treated a thorn scratch, which infected and led to gangrene; the absurdity here is of dying of a little scratch, and of that coming, not while trying to kill game, but while only trying to photograph them. Hemingway begins the story with an epigraph about a leopard carcass dried and frozen near the western summit of Mt. Kilimanjaro. Frozen, preserved, the leopard has achieved a certain immortality while striving to reach the summit, the top. In contrast, Harry is rotting on the plain, both literally and figuratively (here again we have the contrast between mountain and plain that is seen in *A Farewell to Arms*).

Harry's gangrene is linked by Hemingway to a decay of Harry's talent. He has not written his best for years, and in fact came to Africa to "work the fat off his soul the way a fighter went into the mountains to work and train in order to burn it out of his body" (p. 60). His one lament is that, in dying, he will not now be able to write what he has put off writing until he knew enough to do it competently. But then he acknowledges he "would not have to fail at trying to write them either" (p. 54). For years, Harry has lived off rich women as a gigolo, selling himself, using his vitality to live comfortably, rather than to create art. Thus "He had destroyed his talent by not using it, by betrayals of himself and what he believed in" (p. 60). (By writing this fine story, Hemingway makes it difficult for critics to charge that he has wasted his talent as Harry had.)

The stories Harry regrets not having written are presented in italics as heavily edited stream-of-consciousness reminiscences, coldness and snow, for example, uniting memories of Greece, Austria, and World War I service. In their brevity, the essence of the story there, but unelaborated, they are like the interchapters of *In Our Time*.

Harry realizes that death need not make a grand entrance but can come quietly, unobtrusively, like two French bicycle policemen, or a hyena, "not as a rush of water nor of wind; but a sudden evil-smelling emptiness" (p. 64). He blames his wife for his dilemma. She is patient and long-suffering, a romantic who believes "you can't die if you don't give up" (p. 53), obviously untrue. In his self-disgust, Harry is projecting his anger onto her, calling her a rich bitch and blaming the easy life that she has made possible as the reason that he has stopped writing. But he realizes that is not true:

It was not her fault that when he went to her he was already over. . . .
. . . Each day of not writing, of comfort, of being that which he despised, dulled his ability and softened his will to work so that, finally, he did no work at all. (p. 59)

Thus Harry, unlike Manuel Garcia of "The Undefeated" or the leopard of the story's epigraph, is both destroyed and defeated, self-defeated. Gangrene destroys him, but he has not striven to maintain his craft to the best of his ability, he has not maintained self-control and self-discipline. And the decay of his body is the objective correlative, the natural symbol, of that artistic degeneration.

The conclusion of the story mimics in form Ambrose Bierce's story "An Occurrence at Owl Creek Bridge." Harry wakes in the morning believing that a plane has come to take him to Nairobi (as one had taken Hemingway when he had suffered dysentery). On the trip, the pilot flies toward the summit of Mt. Kilimanjaro, "great, high, and unbelievably white in the sun. . . . And then he knew that that was where he was going." But the entire plane flight and the belief that he has deserved the implied immortality that the summit of Kilimanjaro confers are delusions, Harry's last imaginative visions immediately before death.

In October 1940, Hemingway published *For Whom the Bell Tolls* and recouped his standing among critics after it had fallen with *Death in the Afternoon, The Green Hills of Africa, To Have and Have Not,* and *The Fifth Column. For Whom the Bell Tolls* was enormously successful, selling nearly 200,000 copies by year's end. It is a novel based on the Spanish Civil War of 1936–39, which Hemingway saw as the first act of the free world's fight against Fascism; the defeat of the Republicans by Nationalist, Fascist forces,[5] was very ominous for Hemingway, and by the time the novel was completed and published, World War II had indeed begun in Europe. Like *Farewell to Arms, For Whom the Bell Tolls* combines a love story, an adventure story, and an attack on war.

The basic plot concerns three full days in the life of Robert Jordan, an American, a Spanish instructor at the University of Montana, in Spain and fighting on the Loyalist side. He has been active behind Nationalist lines as a dynamiter, working with guerrilla bands to disrupt Nationalist forces. The Republicans plan an attack through the Guadarrama Mountain range toward Segovia, and Jordan is sent to blow up a bridge over which the Nationalists might send reinforcements. He is guided into the mountains by Anselmo to the band of Pablo, a once-fierce fighter now sinking into drink and fear. Pablo's band contains a gypsy named Rafael, brothers Andres and Eladio, Primitivo, Fernando, and Augustín. In Pablo's decay, the band is held together by the woman he lives with, Pilar, Hemingway's most fully realized woman character and a marvelous creation by any standards. The last member of the band is Maria, a girl whom the guerrillas rescued after dynamiting a train she was being transported on. Maria was the daughter of a town mayor who had been shot by the Falangists, and Maria had been raped by Nationalist soldiers. She and Jordan fall in love, very promptly—she enters his sleeping bag the night they meet—and although it might be argued that she commits herself to life and love as Catherine does in *Farewell to Arms,* it is less convincingly an adult act of commitment and more the creation, on Hemingway's part, of a female object of wish fulfillment.

Throughout the novel, Hemingway makes it clear that alignment with an army is frequently less a matter of political choice than of geography or chance of employment. A Spanish young man had to join the union in order to get a job as streetcar conductor; thus the Nationalists considered him a labor radical and executed him and his wife. Once an army controls a territory, all within that area must belong to that army or die, regardless of personal beliefs. Similarly, although Hemingway was sympathetic with the Loyalist, Republican cause, he attacks the brutality on both sides and the absurdity of war as an institution.

The Spanish Civil War was the first mechanized, modern war that involved the wholesale terrorization and destruction of civilians, the German bombing of Guernica (the inspiration of Picasso's painting) being only the most notorious example. Maria's crime, the reason for her parents' execution and her multiple rape, was the party her father belonged to. Andrés, crossing the lines to deliver a message from Jordan, encounters both anarchists who would rather kill him than talk with him, and officers who think that since he comes from Fascist territory, he must be a Fascist. In one of the most riveting, and revolting, sections of the novel, Hemingway has Pilar recount Pablo's taking of their common village. First he lays siege to the military barracks and, after capturing it, executes all survivors. Then he organizes all Loyalists in the village into two lines extending from city hall to a cliff at the edge of the city's plaza, the men in the lines holding flails, pruning hooks, and clubs. His plan is to force the Fascists, defined as store- and landowners, through the gauntlet, to be beaten and then tossed off the cliff, so that all men in the town share in the guilt of their executions. The military strike degenerates into butchery, and that brutality is then revisited on the Republicans when the Nationalists retake the town three days later. Pablo also blinds a captured policeman to make guarding him easier (p. 219), yet that is the side Jordan is fighting on, for the sake of justice and liberty. Jordan, himself, although he comes to help the Loyalists, realizes that while his presence may be of ultimate benefit (might have been if the Loyalists had won), he is often a source of immediate harm. As a guerrilla, Jordan realizes that

you stayed with a peasant and his family. You came at night and ate with them. In the day you were hidden and the next night you were gone. You did your job and cleared out. The next time you came that way you heard that they had been shot. It was as simple as that. (p. 135)

At the end of the novel, Jordan realizes that the Rebels know of the Loyalists' impending attack and sends Andrés to call off what will be a futile waste of life. But Andrés encounters so much stupidity, ignorance, bureaucratic inefficiency, and personal one-upmanship at the cost of cooperation that he is delayed until the very start of the battle, and then no one in the vicinity has the authority to call off the worthless attack without getting Madrid's approval, and there isn't time to do that. Meanwhile, Pablo kills fellow Republicans, allies in the attack on the bridge, so that his band will have enough horses to escape, extra horses they no longer need since several of their number have been killed. Thus Jordan and others in the band give their lives for the cause, nobly, but futilely, and Hemingway scathingly indicts the conduct of both sides, as of war itself.

Also wonderful in the novel is the sense that Hemingway gives that his characters are speaking Spanish throughout, which the author is giving the reader in an accented translation. Literally translating, Hemingway gives the reader "thous" and "thees," as well as "you," distinguishing between colloquial and formal address; he also gives the reader slightly stilted dialogue, but one with remarkable rhythms:

"This is shameful. I have nothing against him but such a spectacle must terminate." So he walked down the line and pushed through to where Don Federico was standing and said, "With your permission," [Spanish *con permiso*] and hit him a great blow alongside the head with a club. (p. 110)

"If I were in the ring with [a bull] now I do not know if I could dominate my legs." (p. 134)

"I will respond for thy material." (p. 259)

Similarly, Hemingway makes an advantage of the era's restriction on the publication of certain four-letter words and gives a sense of great exoticism to the swearing, by quoting some in Spanish, translating some portions literally, but substituting "obscenity" for the actual term in others. For example: "I besmirch the milk of thy duty. . . . I obscenity in the milk of thy tiredness. . . . I befoul myself in the milk of the springtime" (pp. 92–93). And again he twice attempts to capture in prose the rhythm and the tension and release of intercourse (pp. 159, 379), the first passage ending with the much-quoted line about the earth moving.

Although Jordan is given to long and garrulous passages of stream-of-consciousness reminiscence and reflection, many passages in the novel are among the best prose Hemingway ever wrote. He makes the gypsy Rafael describe the dynamiting of a train, and he keeps the language at Rafael's uneducated level, yet marvelously descriptive:

The train was coming steadily. We saw it far away. And I had an excitement so great I cannot tell it. . . . Then it came chu-chu-chu-chu-chu-chu steadily larger and larger and then, at the moment of the explosion, the front wheels of the engine rose up and all of the earth seemed to rise in a great cloud of blackness and a roar

and the engine rose high in the cloud of dirt . . . and then it fell
onto its side like a great wounded animal and there was an explosion of white steam before the clods of the other explosion had
ceased to fall on us and the *máquina* commenced to speak "Ta!
Ta! Tat! Tat! Tat! Ta!" (p. 29)

Pilar's whole description of Pablo's attack on her village
and her account of the smell of death, as well as Hemingway's narrative of the death of Sordo, another guerrilla
leader, are all tours de force, superb examples of narrative,
too long to quote here in their entireties, but comparable to
Rafael's account in excellence. Another prose technique
well handled is the intercutting of chapters between Jordan
and the partisans at the bridge and Andrés's attempt to
reach Loyalist headquarters. Will Andrés get there in time
to prevent the attack, will Jordan have to blow the bridge
with makeshift equipment, will there be enough of them to
subdue the guard posts? Almost cinematically, Hemingway
cuts back and forth between the two events, heightening
tension by progressively shortening Andrés's chapters.

As I have said, the conversion of Maria from ravaged victim to dedicated lover is abrupt and, on retrospect, uncon-
vincing. In context, however, Hemingway almost makes the
reader believe; he marvelously reestablishes Maria's innocence when he has her say to Jordan that she would like to
kiss him but does not know how: "Where do the noses go?
I have always wondered where the noses would go?" (p.
71). He individualizes each of the characters, distinguishing
the foul-mouthed Agustín from the pompous Fernando; he
shows the dignity of an old man like Anselmo who delights
in hunting animals, but who cries when he must shoot his
fellow man, even though they are the enemy; he scrutinizes
the courage of Andrés, the "bulldog of Villaconejos" and
through Andrés of all men: Andrés is always first in attacking the bull in his village's amateur bullfights, but he is se-
cretly relieved to be delivering a message for Jordan rather
than attacking the bridge. And Hemingway makes Pilar
fully dimensional, strong, where Pablo is weak, yet tender
toward him, pushing Maria into Jordan's sleeping bag for

the girl's sake, knowing that she must love to become whole again, and yet jealous of Maria's beauty and of the happiness of the young lovers. Her complexity is marvelously represented. Through Pablo's default, she is the band's leader. When the partisans agree to help Jordan, in spite of Pablo's objections, she tells him:

"Here I command! Haven't you heard *la gente* [the people]? Here no one commands but me. You can stay if you wish and eat of the food and drink of the wine, but not too bloody much, and share in the work if thee wishes. But here I command." (p. 55)

This role reversal is taking place, let me insist again, in 1930s' conservative, Catholic Spain, where a woman's place was explicitly defined as secondary to the male's. Later, she takes Jordan and Maria to meet El Sordo, where they encounter Joaquín, a nineteen-year-old failed bullfighter. Teasing him, Pilar says:

"And if Maria kisses thee again I will commence kissing thee myself. It's years since I've kissed a bullfighter, even an unsuccessful one like thee.... Hold him, *Inglés,* till I get a good kiss at him."
"*Deja* [leave it]" the boy said and turned away sharply.
....

"At times many things tire me," Pilar said angrily. "You understand? And one of them is to have forty-eight years. You hear me? Forty-eight years and an ugly face. Another is to see panic in the face of a failed bullfighter of Communist tendencies when I say, as a joke, I might kiss him." (pp. 140–41)

Pilar also embodies, and makes most explicit, dedication and commitment to a cause. In contrast to *Farewell to Arms* and Hemingway's comments about the obscenity of abstract words such as *honor* or *courage,* abstract terms such as *duty, freedom,* and *liberty* are frequent in *For Whom the Bell Tolls,* as well as examples of the need—not for the independence and self-reliance of a Jake Barnes— but for the interdependence and human solidarity of those fighting together for a common cause, recognizing that a man alone has no chance and that no man is an island entire unto himself. Pilar was for years the companion of Finito, a short, tubercular bullfighter, so short, in fact, that he was almost always hit by a bull's horns when he went in for the kill; he knew he would be hit with the flat of the bull's horns as the bull charged by, yet he killed the bull calmly, accepting the inevitable pain and, ostensibly, ultimately dying from the repeated injuries to his chest. Pilar eulogizes him thus:

"He was short of stature and he had a thin voice and much fear of bulls. Never have I seen a man with more fear before the bullfight and never have I seen a man with less fear in the ring. You," she said to Pablo. "You are afraid to die now. You think that is something of importance. But Finito was afraid all the time and in the ring he was like a lion." (p. 185)

Pilar is part gypsy and skillful at palm reading. She reads Jordan's palm and sees death there as a result of the mission they will undertake. (It isn't important whether Hemingway believed in palm reading; it is important that the gypsy Pilar believes her own gifts, and the way she acts as a result.) In spite of her belief that Jordan and the mission are doomed, and possibly herself as well, she pushes Maria at Jordan, commits herself and the men in her band to Jordan's mission: " 'I am for the Republic,' the woman of Pablo said happily. 'And the Republic is the bridge' " (p. 53). Later, Maria tells Jordan, "The Pilar told me that we would all die tomorrow and that you know it as well as she does and that you give it no importance. She said this not in criticism but in admiration" (p. 345).

The Hemingway code includes doing what one can as well as one can, regardless of what befalls one, with skill, determination, and craftsmanship. This is what Pilar admires in Jordan, and she displays the same qualities even more herself. Initially Jordan is not pessimistic about his chances, but after the death of Sordo, he grows increasingly so, and thinks about his grandfather's courage fighting in the American Civil War and against the Indians thereafter; he also thinks of his father's suicide, and how he himself will measure up to his forebears. Ultimately, he demonstrates the courage that Pilar has modeled for him.

At one point in the novel a Nationalist cavalryman rides into the guerrillas' camp, and Jordan shoots him. Reading the boy's letters, Jordan discovers him to be from Tafalla, "twenty-one years old, unmarried, and the son of a blacksmith. . . . I've probably seen him run through the streets ahead of the bulls at the Feria in Pamplona, Robert Jordan thought. You never kill any one that you want to kill in a war" (p. 302). The boy has sewn on his uniform the Sacred Heart of Jesus, given him by his sister, who insists that it has been "proven innumerable . . . times to have the power of stopping bullets." Of course it doesn't stop Jordan's, and Maria accuses him of having shot at it. Both sides pray to the same God, same Virgin, same saints. Joaquín, when Sordo's band is attacked, begins spouting Communist slogans and then shifts to prayer. The Nationalist officer, Paco Berrendo, who administers the coup de grace to Joaquín, "made the sign of the cross and then shot him in the back of the head." Hemingway makes Berrendo intelligent, religious, and human. And although it revolts him, Berrendo then cuts off the heads of Sordo's troop as evidence of their death. At the end of the novel, Jordan, lying behind a tree with his leg broken, has Paco Berrendo in his gunsights.

By concentrating the events of the novel into three days, Hemingway strove for the compression of Greek tragedy and, for the most part, achieved it. *For Whom the Bell Tolls* is a great novel of romance and war; a paean to enjoying life while one can, for the time of everyone is limited; a testimony to human courage; and a denunciation of war and man's inhumanity to man. And, published as it was in 1940, a year after World War II had begun in Europe, it was his trumpet call to Americans in the battle against Fascism.

5

≈≈≈≈≈≈≈≈≈≈≈≈≈≈≈≈≈≈≈≈≈≈≈≈≈≈≈≈≈≈≈≈≈≈≈≈≈≈≈

Up to the End

During the war years Hemingway did little publishing: in 1942 he selected stories for soldiers in a thousand-page book called *Men at War*, and he wrote war correspondence for *Collier's* magazine in the latter half of 1944. In his rambling introduction to *Men at War*, Hemingway stated bluntly his antipathy for war:

The editor of this anthology . . . hates war and hates all the politicians whose mismanagement, gullibility, cupidity, selfishness, and ambition brought on this present war and made it inevitable. But once we have a war there is only one thing to do. It must be won. For defeat brings worse things than any that can ever happen in a war.[1]

His purpose in compiling the volume, Hemingway stated, was to show to those who have to endure a war that others have done so before them, faced what they must, and acquitted themselves with courage. He wanted to give combatants accounts of others like themselves, for when he had been a naive youth in World War I, he "would have given anything for a book . . . which showed what all the other men we are a part of had gone through and how it had been with them" (pp. xii–xiii). "Whatever I had to do [in combat] men had always done. If they had done it then I could do it too and the best thing was not to worry about it" (p. xii).

In selecting stories for the *Men at War* anthology, Hemingway was guided by the principal of truth, the truth of war as he knew it, obviously, rather than literary merit alone, fine writing on the subject of war. He rejected several suggestions of the publisher as exaggerated and fanciful, clinging to the eyewitness observer or the account, though fictional, that smacked of truth.

A writer's job is to tell the truth. His standard of fidelity to the truth should be so high that his invention, out of his experience, should produce a truer account than anything factual can be. For facts can be observed badly; but when a good writer is creating something, he has time and scope to make it of an absolute truth.

Screaming, necessary though it may be to attract attention at the time, reads badly in later years. (pp. xiv,xv)

(The reader sees again the importance of craft for him, whether the skill and courage of the writer or the skill and courage of a soldier under fire.) By his definition of what constituted true writing, he includes accounts from the Bible of David's battle with Goliath and Joshua's conquest of Jericho, Virgil's account of the Trojan Horse from the *Aeneid*, along with historical accounts of the Crusades. Eyewitness accounts, such as Stendhal's of Waterloo, are represented, as are fictional ones, Stephen Crane's account of the Civil War in *The Red Badge of Courage*. Hemingway includes three of his own works: the retreat from Caporetto from *Farewell to Arms*, Sordo's last stand from *For Whom the Bell Tolls*, and a slight short story (mostly journalism) from the Spanish Civil War called "The Chauffeurs of Madrid" (which was not kept in the paperback reprint and has never been reprinted since). He mixed authors noted for their literary style—Victor Hugo, Tolstoy, Winston Churchill, Ambrose Bierce, and Faulkner—with such individuals, now unknown to us, as Mary Johnson, Private 19022, and Blake Clark. Although World War II was at its fury when the book was first published, and it concludes with accounts of Pearl Harbor and the Battle of Midway, Hemingway prefaces sections with quotations from the German military strategist General Karl von Clausewitz, and he also includes, as testimony to their courage, an account of the Japanese naval victory during the Russo-Japanese

War. War he hated, but the accounts of brave men, regardless of their nation, he admired.

After the war, he did two brief introductions, for John Groth's *Studio: Europe* and for another anthology *A Treasury of the Free World*. In 1946, he began writing *The Garden of Eden*, which was not published until 1986. Although he returned to the manuscript several times over the years, he never finished it. In 1948, in Italy, he met eighteen-year-old Adriana Ivancich while shooting birds on a private estate and promptly became infatuated. Soon he put aside his lengthy novel of the land, sea, and air to write a novel inspired by Adriana and Venice. (Adriana was always well chaperoned, usually by her mother, when she and Hemingway were together in Italy or in visits to him in Cuba; Mary Hemingway was also present, controlling her jealousy. Hemingway loved the girl as a symbol of his youth, as the daughter he had long wished for and never had, and as the attractive woman that she was. She was flattered by the attention of an older man, one who was world-famous, but she did not reciprocate his passion and there seems never to have been an affair.) The resulting novel, *Across the River and into the Trees* (1950), is probably Hemingway's worst. Critics have tried to redeem it from its own failings, praising the denseness of allusion to such writers as Dante, Thomas Mann (*Death in Venice*), and Gabriele D'Annunzio, the symbolic resonance of nearly every scene, every word, but none of these make the novel work.

The book recounts the last days of a Colonel, formerly General, Richard Cantwell, who is stationed in Trieste after World War II and returns to Venice to spend a last weekend before his imminent death, a Venice he fought for and protected in World War I. The title of the novel comes from the dying words of Confederate General Stonewall Jackson, and as critic Philip Young points out, they constitute a metaphor for the land of death.[2] The colonel has suffered three heart attacks and knows that death is near and tries to prepare for it, while enjoying life to the fullest: seeing his mistress; enjoying food, wine, and companionship; and duck shooting. Like Hemingway, Cantwell is fifty-one, was

wounded in Italy in World War I, was an observer in the
Spanish Civil War, and was in the Huertgen Campaign of
World War II. Like Hemingway, Cantwell was married and
divorced and now has a nearly nineteen-year-old girlfriend
of Italian nobility; unlike Hemingway's situation, the colonel's girlfriend returns his passion. The colonel is taking ni-
troglycerin for his angina, and like Stonewall Jackson,
Cantwell also was shot through the hand (Cantwell, twice),
as well as having been wounded in the head, chest, and leg.
With his wound in his hand and pain in his side, the colonel is a Christ figure; he is also Richard the Lion-Hearted
and "Mister Dante" (pp. 229, 246). The girlfriend, Renata, is Cantwell's Beatrice (Dante's heroine and inspiration); Renata means rebirth. She gives the colonel a gift of
sea green emeralds, as the Doge of Venice gives a ring to
the sea, marrying Venice to the water; so the opposites in
the book are married: age and youth, experience and innocence, male and female, land and water, love and war, etc.
Renata is Catholic and will not marry the colonel because
he has been married before. She seeks to purge the colonel
of his bitterness (as in purgatory), to allow him a good
death, shriven and forgiven: "I want you to die with the
grace of a happy death" (p. 240). The intentions of the
novel may be admirable; the effect is not.

The colonel's name: Cant-well. Does it apply to his heart
condition, the fact that he can no longer exert himself well?
Yet the colonel, in his reminiscences, says that he was an
exceptional soldier, fighting bravely, only losing men by following the orders of unknowing desk jockeys. He shoots
well at duck hunting, and—in spite of the heart condition
that pains him after walking over a Venetian bridge and
that kills him—he knocks out two sailors in a street brawl
because they have whistled at Renata and show no respect
to him or his rank, and he makes love to her three times in
a gondola (no lack of ability there). Moreover, he knows
literature (alluding to Dante, Shakespeare, Blake, Whitman,
Rimbaud, Verlaine, and Eliot), art, history, and gourmet
foods and wines; his joy of life is such that "he had never
been sad one waking morning of his life" (p. 289). What

then is it that he can't well? Why is his comic-book-reading driver named Jackson, the same as General Stonewall Jackson? Obviously there is a contrast between those who do their jobs well, thoroughly, artistically, and with dignity, whether soldier, waiter, or gondolier; but that contrast between the colonel and his driver is apparent without the name Jackson.

Hemingway has the colonel drop names: George Patton, Erwin Rommel (with whom the Colonel skied after they had fought on opposite sides in World War I), Bernard Montgomery, Charles Leclerc, Dwight Eisenhower (a "Politician General," not yet elected president when the novel was published) and, by allusion, Harry S. Truman. He makes Cantwell a latter-day Wild Bill Hickok, counting those he has killed (difficult in these days of mechanized warfare), always concerned that he sit with his back covered and careful to notice each person entering a room, lest someone slip up on him unawares to kill him. Cantwell's desire to be observant is laudable, as is his waking each morning to greet the day, but to be observant only to be aware of potential assassins when one is dying of heart disease seems anachronistic and ludicrous.

The novel is full of talk, rather than action; some duck shooting, a one-page street brawl, and some rather vague lovemaking are the only activities in a 308-page book—the rest is conversation (some of it to Renata's portrait), description, or reminiscence. Much of the colonel's and Renata's conversations have to do with his explaining American slang to her, slang now badly dated. (Perhaps it is this cant that the colonel knows well.) The distance between author and character is not well established. Cantwell seems very close to Hemingway, in age, history, friendships, and dislikes. Cantwell's service in World War II, at least all that he recalls, seems limited to the period from the invasion of Normandy to the Huertgen Campaign, from June 1944 to January 1945, seven months, exactly Hemingway's time covering the front, but certainly not all the service of a field-grade American officer during the entirety of the war. Cantwell calls Renata "daughter," as Hemingway was then addressing women, notably in Lillian Ross's profile of him for the *New Yorker* (May 13, 1950). The colonel and Renata mock Sinclair Lewis unmercifully (by description, not by name); Lewis, who had praised Hemingway when accepting the Nobel Prize twenty years before in 1930, was in Venice when Hemingway was. Perhaps saddest is the self-parody of what had once been Hemingway's tight, bare-bones prose, with only the telling detail. Instead this novel gives us inflated, meaningless rhetoric: "Please put your arms around me. Gently and well" (p. 114); gently, yes, but what does "well" mean in that context? On the same page, the colonel's "heart [is] broken, honestly and fairly." Renata "chewed well and solidly on her steak" (p. 127). After making love to Renata, the colonel reached "accurately and well for the champagne bucket" (p. 154), and while dying he still manages to close the car door, "carefully and well" (p. 307). For an author once extremely chary of adjectives and adverbs, Hemingway's use of them in *Across the River* seems careless and slapdash. Hemingway tells the reader when the characters are speaking Spanish or Italian, unlike the lilting suggestions of it in *The Sun Also Rises* or *For Whom the Bell Tolls* with their stilted constructions suggesting literal translation of a foreign tongue or the presence of non-English words. Instead, in this novel, the reader gets, " 'It was easy,' the Colonel told her in Italian."

If we are to lament the Colonel's death, Hemingway does not give us enough of his life to care. If one is to admire Renata's gentling of his "wild boar blood" again, one is not given enough of an interest in the colonel to care. He seems, in fact, rather fortunate, living in one of Venice's most expensive hotels, dining off lobster and champagne, with a young girlfriend giving him emeralds, his death no tragedy. Limiting the novel to a long weekend does not achieve the compression of *For Whom the Bell Tolls,* nor does the relationship of the lovers achieve the intensity of Robert and Maria's, so the separation is not as painful; in fact, the age and life-style difference, the chattiness of the novel, and the flaccidity of the prose undermine it further. It is not a good novel, and the critics tore it and its author apart.

Adriana Ivancich (and her mother) visited Hemingway (and Mary) in Cuba in late October 1950, taking some of the sting out of the reviews. Inspired, Hemingway returned to his large sea novel, the adventures of Thomas Hudson, what was later published as *Islands in the Stream*. In the new year, he turned his attention to the story he had told briefly in *Esquire* in April 1936 of a Cuban fisherman towed to sea by a giant marlin, and finished the first draft of *The Old Man and the Sea* by mid-February. He also wrote two fables for *Holiday*, "The Good Lion" and "The Faithful Bull," an introduction to a bibliography of his works, and a preface to *Pourqoui Ces Bêtes Sont-elles Sauvages?*, a picture book of African wildlife, and returned to Thomas Hudson's story.

The Old Man and the Sea was published September 1, 1952, in a single issue of *Life* magazine (the first time that *Life* had ever published a whole novella) and as a Book-of-the-Month-Club selection a week later; the magazine version sold five million copies in two days, and still the book sales went well. Hemingway's reputation was definitely restored. *The Old Man and the Sea* is a parable about human existence, and as a parable, moving though it is, it lacks human depth and complexity. Hemingway had considered "The Dignity of Man" as a title, but thought it, while accurate, too pompous.[3] The story tells of an old Cuban fisherman who has gone eighty-four days without catching a major fish. On noon of the eighty-fifth day he catches a giant, eighteen-foot-long, 1,500 pound marlin, which tows him farther out to sea for two more days, only coming close enough to be killed on the third day. The old man, Santiago, lashes the fish to his skiff—it is too big to fit into the boat—and sails back to the fishing port of Cojimar, near Havana; along the way, sharks attack the bleeding marlin and strip all the meat from it, despite the efforts of the old man to prevent them. It is a simple story, told in a style close to original Hemingway prose, replete with meanings. And though Hemingway was at pains to deny any overt symbolism, it is obviously present and at one time, at least, too painfully obvious.

To begin with, there are Biblical and specifically Christian images. Santiago is more than twice the Biblical "forty days" without a fish (p. 9). Santiago is the Spanish form of St. James, the Galilean fisherman apostle of Jesus, and martyr. At the end of the novella, having been scourged by the rope across his back, having been cut around the eye, having his hand stigmatized by line cuts, Santiago shoulders his mast, as Christ did His Cross, stumbles under its weight as he carries it, and falls asleep on his bed in the cruciform position. For those for whom these are not obvious enough to show how Santiago is Christ-like in his endurance of the pain of life, Hemingway, when Santiago sees the second sharks, adds, " 'Ay,' he said aloud. There is no translation for this word and perhaps it is just a noise such as a man might make, involuntarily, feeling the nail go through his hands and into the wood" (p. 107).

Within such a specifically Christian context, it is appropriate to see the fish as *ichthys,* the symbol of the early Christians, based on the Greek words "Jesus Christ, Son of God, the Savior," whose initials form as an acrostic the word *ichthys,* or fish. And as Hemingway has done with Santiago, the fish is also identified with Christ and His Passion. The fish goes down to the depths for three days and ascends on the third. Santiago spears the fish in its side, "just behind the great chest fin that rose high in the air to the altitude of a man's chest" (p. 94). The subsequent paragraph—"Then the fish came alive, with his death in him, and rose high out of the water showing all his great length and width and all his power and beauty. He seemed to hang in the air above the old man"—echoes the earlier "all his greatness and glory" (p. 66), and both echo the Lord's Prayer: "For Thine is the kingdom and the power and the glory."

Hemingway identifies hunter and hunted, killer and prey. Throughout the novella, Santiago calls the fish his brother, so the fact that both are identified with Christ should not be confusing: both suffer, both endure, both act nobly. Both show how one should act under duress. "You are killing me, fish, the old man thought. But you have a right to. Never have I seen a greater, or more beautiful, or a calmer or more noble thing than you, brother" (p. 92).

Although Santiago is alone for most of the novel, Hemingway is at pains to make him the center of several concentric circles of connectedness to others. First, there is the boy, Manolin, the old man's surrogate son and disciple, whom he has initiated into the craft of fishing. Then there is the community of fishermen and friends who support him, giving him food, bait, and credit. Beyond that, there is the human community, which searches for the old man when he is missing, " 'with coast guard and with planes'. . . . 'The ocean is very big and a skiff is small and hard to see,' the old man said. He noticed how pleasant it was to have someone to talk to instead of speaking only to himself and to the sea" (p. 124). In fact, throughout his ordeal, Santiago has prayed for Manolin's presence—his help, his youth, as if Santiago could share it, and his company. But the fisherman is a member of communities more than human; Hemingway makes Santiago at one with all of nature, and not just his prey:

He knew no man was ever alone on the sea.   (p. 61)

He was very fond of flying fish as they were his principal friends on the ocean. He was sorry for the birds, especially the small delicate dark terns . . .   (p. 29)

He loved green turtles and hawk-bills. . . . Most people are heartless about turtles because a turtle's heart will beat for hours after he has been cut up and butchered. But the old man thought, I have such a heart too and my feet and hands are like theirs.   (p. 37)

He eats turtle eggs, though, and drinks shark liver oil, not only for the nourishment provided, but also—as he will later do to the flesh of the marlin—as an act of ritual "at-onement," of ingesting the qualities of another, of communion.

What all these creatures share is an indifferent universe. A migrating warbler perches on the line between Santiago and the marlin. " 'Take a good rest, small bird,' he said. 'Then go in and take your chance like any man or bird or fish' " (p. 55). The message here is one the reader has encountered before: a cruel, indifferent world, where an individual creates his own code of conduct and is measured against it. Santiago is a fisherman and prides himself on the skill, the craft, with which he conducts his profession:

Each bait hung head down with the shank of the hook inside the bait fish, tied and sewed solid and all the projecting part of the hook . . . was covered with fresh sardines. . . . (p. 31)

He kept [his lines] straighter than anyone did, so that at each level in the darkness of the stream there would be a bait waiting exactly where he wished it to be for any fish that swam there. Others let them drift with the current and sometimes they were at sixty fathoms when the fishermen thought they were at a hundred.

But, he thought, I keep them with precision. Only I have no luck any more. . . . It is better to be lucky. But I would rather be exact. (p. 32)

Man cannot control fate, what destiny gives to him; we are back with *The Sun Also Rises* and the saying from Ecclesiastes that the race is not always to the swift, nor the battle to the strong, but that time and chance happen to all men (Ecc. 9:11). What man can do, must do, in the face of adversity is maintain his own standards of conduct and endure. "Although it is unjust, he thought. But I will show [the fish] what a man can do and what a man endures. . . . The thousand times he had proved it meant nothing. Now he was proving it again" (p. 66). After three days at sea, his hands badly cut, Santiago works to bring the marlin in close enough to harpoon him: "He took all his pain and what was left of his strength and his long gone pride and he put it against the fish's agony" (p. 93).

There is a certain reflexiveness in Hemingway's description of Santiago, his care with his craft, and his efforts. Just as Romero's "straight and pure and natural in line" in *The Sun Also Rises* could apply equally well to Hemingway's prose, so too Santiago's lines, "as thick around as a big pencil" (p. 31), which he kept "straighter than any one" (p. 32). And with each new book, Hemingway, and the critics, felt that he had to prove himself again.

Santiago fights the sharks as long as he is able, protecting his catch:

He hit [the shark] with his blood mushed hands driving a good harpoon with all his strength. He hit it without hope but with resolution and complete malignancy. (p. 102)

That shark takes Santiago's harpoon with him. The old man kills two more sharks with his knife lashed to an oar, but the knife blade breaks on the second shark. "Now they have beaten me, he thought. I am too old to club sharks to death. But I will try as long as I have oars and the short club and the tiller" (p. 112). "I'll fight them until I die" (p. 115). And fight them he does, until weapons and marlin are gone. In this book, Hemingway does not leave the message to be deduced. He states it explicitly: "A man can be destroyed but not defeated" (p. 103). Bad luck, fate, may destroy a man, but if he maintains his own standards, he will maintain his dignity and not be defeated—a romantic notion for someone considered, as Hemingway has been, a nihilist.

Aristotle insists that Greek tragic heroes contribute to their misfortunes, and Santiago does so in losing the marlin to the sharks, and does so in ways suggestive of Greek tragedy. When Manolin asks him where he intends to fish, Santiago answers, "Far out." Having caught the marlin, he reflects, "His choice had been to stay in deep water far out beyond all snares and traps and treacheries. My choice was to go there to find him beyond all people. Beyond all the people in the world." And at novel's end, he thinks: "And what beat you. . . . 'Nothing,' he said aloud. 'I went out too far.'"

Santiago commits hubris, an act of presumption or arrogance—to go beyond others, to achieve more, and thereby establish oneself as better, and thus links himself with such Greek heroes as Achilles and Oedipus. Hemingway repeats a paradox here, one discussed by philosopher Friedrich Nietzsche in *The Birth of Tragedy:* without exceeding the common norm, nothing exceptional is accomplished, but by going beyond others one invites criticism and punishment. Santiago goes out far, catches his fish, and then is punished for his hubris by having the flesh stripped off his prize. He returns only with the skeleton. But his fellow fishermen know from its length that Santiago is still *El Campeon,* still able, still capable, still a master fisherman. That they alone know explains the misunderstanding between tourist and waiter at the novella's end: the tourists, the uninitiated, are uncomprehending (echoing Mark 4:12).

Just as Jake emulates the sports hero Romero, so too does Santiago have a hero he measures himself against, also from sports, but with a difference. Santiago's hero is Joe DiMaggio, who played baseball for the New York Yankees when the novella was written but who had retired by the time of publication because of his advanced age: thirty-seven years. DiMaggio, like the fictional Romero, was a skilled craftsman who made his art look easy. He was troubled with growths on his heel, bone spurs, which required surgery, and Santiago, struggling to bring in his fish with cuts on his hands, compares himself and his pain to that of DiMaggio, old for his occupation and also physically hampered. There is one significant difference between Romero and DiMaggio, though. A bullfighter faces the bull essentially alone. Boxers like Ole Andreson and Jack Brennan also face their opponents alone. The shift toward greater social concern and awareness that Hemingway had begun in the thirties with *To Have and Have Not* and *For Whom the Bell Tolls* is continued here with the concentric circling of societies and even in the choice of a hero to emulate. Baseball is a team sport, and DiMaggio was the quintessential team player, sparking the team and encouraging their efforts. So Santiago thinks of Joe DiMaggio, whose father was a fisherman, wondering if he measures up to his hero, and he dreams of lions, the only cats who are social, grouping in packs, and he wishes that Manolin were with him. At the end, Manolin nurses him and waits for Santiago to heal so that he may accompany his hero and continue learning from him.

The novella is, as I said, essentially a parable of the need for human connection and for a self-defined code of conduct that measures the individual, fate notwithstanding; and as such, it does not deal with psychology or human complexity. Santiago does speculate, but his philosophizing is neither deep nor convincing:

> Imagine if each day a man must try to kill the moon, he thought. The moon runs away. But imagine if a man each day should have to try to kill the sun? We were born lucky, he thought. (p. 75)

Such ramblings are, however, minimal, even less than in *For Whom the Bell Tolls*. And the prose, while it no longer struck the audience of literary critics with the force Hemingway's prose had in the twenties—and some critics accused him of imitating himself—was sparser and cleaner, with fewer ill-placed adverbs than that of *Across the River and into the Trees*. However thin and obvious it might have been, *The Old Man and the Sea* was good reading, showed that Hemingway could still tell a story and control his prose, and had not lost his talent. In fact, he won the Pulitzer Prize for literature the following year, 1953, and the Nobel Prize the year after. He would have won in 1953 for his complete works, especially *The Old Man and the Sea*, but the prize was supposed to go to works of moral uplift, idealistic works, and the Prize Committee was disturbed, as the award announcement said when it did come, by Hemingway's "brutal, cynical, and callous" early prose; the 1953 award for literature went to Winston Churchill. Nevertheless, fearing to have lost Hemingway after his 1954 plane crashes, the committee acknowledged his oeuvre, his "heroic pathos" and his "powerful style-making mastery of the art of modern narration, most recently displayed in *The Old Man and the Sea,* and for his influence on contemporary style," awarding him the 1954 Nobel Prize.

Hemingway's only writing in the midfifties was a two-part article for *Look* magazine of his safari and plane crashes.[4] The first part is factual and mildly amusing; the second is garrulous. He and Mary visited Europe in 1956, and while in Paris, the management of the Ritz Hotel informed Hemingway that there were trunks of his in the basement, stored since 1928. Browsing through the trunks revealed notebooks from the early days in Paris and reminded Hemingway of the beginnings of his career, or so, at least, Hemingway claimed (see footnote 4, chapter 1). A request by the *Atlantic* for a memoir of Scott Fitzgerald further stimulated him to write about his own early days in Paris. During this same period Hemingway wrote a series of short stories, including some about World War II experiences (now in the Finca Vigía edition of *The Complete Short Stories of Ernest Hemingway*), and gave two bad stories to the *Atlantic*—"A Man of the World" and "Get Yourself a Seeing-Eyed Dog"[5]—in place of the Fitzgerald memoir, which he kept for *A Moveable Feast.* He finished that body of recollections and delivered a draft of the manuscript to Scribner's in March 1959.

That same year, *Life* Magazine commissioned him to do a ten-thousand-word story to accompany photos taken by a *Life* photographer of a contest between Spain's two best bullfighters: Louis Miguel Dominguín, who had retired from bullfighting in 1953, and Antonio Ordóñez, son of Cayetano Ordóñez, Hemingway's model for Pedro Romero in *The Sun Also Rises.* To complicate the rivalry, Ordóñez was married to Dominguín's sister and managed by Dominguín's brothers. Hemingway went to Spain for the summer fights, adopted Ordóñez as his protégé, and adopted a biased view of the fighters as a result. Hemingway acknowledged that Dominguín was technically knowledgeable and proficient, and perhaps the best banderillero in Spain—Or-

dóñez did not place his own banderillas—but complained
that Dominguín's capework did not excite him or move
him. Moreover, he criticized, as he had in *Death in the Afternoon*, the decadence of bullfighting, the tricks that had
entered for the amusement and entertainment of the audience, at the expense of the art of bullfighting—tricks such
as leaning against the bull's head, pretending to be receiv-
ing a telephone call—and he accused both Dominguín and
Spain's national hero, the bullfighter Manolete, of such
tricks, earning the intense enmity of Spanish readers.

Hemingway took notes during the summer and wrote
them up afterward, beginning in October. He could not
now control his garrulousness. What was supposed to have
been a ten-thousand-word journalistic account, accompanied by photographs, constituting an appendix and updat-
ing of *Death in the Afternoon*, grew into a book of over
one-hundred-thousand words by May 1960, much of it
slack and tedious. Hemingway himself was unable to cut
his own manuscript. He asked Aaron Hotchner to do the
editing, and together they cut the text in late June and early
July to sixty-thousand words.[6] The *Life* editors cut it still
more, sometimes with clumsy transitions, and published it
in three installments, September 5, September 12, and September 19, 1960. At its few moments of intensity, describing the matadors in action, it rivals *Death in the Afternoon*,
but it adds no new information about the art of bullfighting nor its symbolic significance for the author; and its moments of intensity are few.

Part 1 is largely nostalgia, reminiscences of Spain, together with appreciation of the landscape, food, and wine.
As a result, together with the editing of the longer narrative, part 1 is choppy and episodic. There is no uniting narrative until the rivalry, the *mano a mano* (hand-to-hand)
contest between the bullfighters begins. In part 2, Hemingway throughout arrogates to himself not only knowledge of
bullfighting that it seems only an active participant, not
just an observer, would have, but knowledge also of the
bull's condition and feelings. Part 3 continues the rivalry,
both matadors being gored, ending the contest. Through-

out, but particularly in part 2, there is also more on the courage, craft, and self-control of the bullfighter, a paradigm of all artists and all individuals who seek aesthetic control in their lives:

> Any man could face death but to be committed to bring it as close as possible while performing certain classic movements and do this again and again and again and then deal it out yourself with a sword to an animal weighing half a ton, which you love, is more complicated than just facing death. It is facing your performance as a creative artist every day and your necessity to function as a skillful killer. (*Life*, September 12, 1960, p. 76)

Hemingway's own lack of control is obvious here. The first sentence is long and confusing. The modification is misplaced: the bullfighter loves the fighting bull, not his half ton of weight. Finally, the rhythm of the prose, which Hemingway had been such a master of, uniting it to the action he is describing, here, does nothing. These three pieces were the last that would be published in Hemingway's lifetime. (*Moveable Feast*, although delivered to Scribner's in 1959 and worried over by Hemingway in the two remaining years of his life, was only published afterward.) They are not, as published, bad writing, but to quote Ezra Pound, they "present no [significant] adjunct to the Muses' diadem."

6

The Posthumous Works

The posthumous works pose problems for general readers who do not have access to the manuscripts in the John F. Kennedy Library in Boston (repository for Hemingway's works), because they have gone to press without Hemingway's personal supervision, inattentive as that sometimes was, and have been edited by others. The editing for *A Moveable Feast* seems minimal, but still problematic; the editing for *The Garden of Eden* eliminated several major characters and some two-thirds of the manuscript text. Thus in dealing with the published texts one has to be very careful in talking about authorial intention, patterns of imagery, etc., because what one has is not directly from the author's hand and not as he may have wanted it to be. *A Moveable Feast* provides an excellent case in point.

Hemingway claimed in late 1956 to have had returned to him by the management of the Ritz Hotel in Paris two trunks of his that had been stored since 1928, trunks containing notebooks from his early days as a writer in Paris, notebooks that stimulated his desire to write his memoirs of those days. (Actually, the published account of finding the trunks is Mary Hemingway's "The Making of a Book: A Chronicle and a Memoir," *New York Times Book Review,* May 10, 1964.) This has been the popularly accepted account of the origin of *A Moveable Feast.* But a Hemingway scholar, Jacqueline Tavernier-Courbin, doubts the account. She can find no convincing evidence in Hemingway's correspondence to his friends, no corroboration from Ritz Hotel employees, and none in Hemingway's known habits (see note 4, chapter 1, p. 139).

So the origin of the book may not be as it has been reported. That, at least, should not affect our reception of the book. But other things do. As I noted in the previous chapter, Hemingway had delivered a manuscript of *A Moveable Feast* to Scribner's in 1959; the published volume differs from that manuscript in significant ways, as Professors Tavernier-Courbin and Brenner have reported.[1] The published version contains a note from Mary Hemingway that says the book was completed in Cuba in 1960, but the manuscript was given to Scribner's in 1959 uncompleted, or at least not in finished form, and there do not seem to be any additions by Ernest after that date. Moreover, Mary says in her autobiography, *How It Was,* "except for punctuation and the obviously overlooked 'ands' and 'buts' we would present his prose and poetry to readers as he wrote it. . . . Where repetitions and redundancies occurred, we would cut. We would not add anything."[2] "We" refers to herself and Scribner's editor L. H. (Harry) Brague, and in spite of the disclaimer of presenting Ernest's works as he had written them, Mary admits a few lines later that she and Brague "switch[ed] about some chapters for continuity's sake," upsetting, in Gerry Brenner's view, patterns of development in the book and close contrasts that had existed in contiguous chapters. Most important, however, Mary added a chapter that had not been in the 1959 manuscript, and she drastically altered a preface, not delivered to Scribner's, but among Hemingway's manuscripts. Hemingway had written:

> This book is fiction. . . . No one can write true fact in reminiscences. . . .
> All remembrance of things past is fiction. . . .
> This book is fiction and should be read as such.[3]

Since *A Moveable Feast* contains such obviously nonfictional characters as Gertrude Stein, Ezra Pound, F. Scott Fitzgerald, and Ernest Hemingway, such a declaration is difficult to entertain. On the one hand, Hemingway provides a way to avoid libel suits, despite the use of actual names, by proclaiming the book as fiction (and Hemingway was worried about libel, as his correspondence with his publisher makes clear). Artistically, he recognizes the fact that all writing distorts, and all autobiographies are works of fiction. Mary's emendation in the published version is more coy, less honest. The published preface reads, "If the reader prefers, this book may be regarded as fiction."[4]

The book is a first-person memoir, a series of reminiscences, and is printed in separately titled chapters rather than as a narrative whole; it recounts Hemingway's early years in Paris, the people he knew, his struggles to become a good writer, and some details about his writing methods. The book's title comes from lines Hemingway wrote to A. E. Hotchner in 1950, lines that are quoted on the title page: "If you are lucky enough to have lived in Paris as a young man, then wherever you go for the rest of your life, it stays with you, for Paris is a moveable feast." The larger-format editions include photographs, and although there is no tight narrative structure, there are connective touches, both of mood and detail. The book begins in medias res, with Hemingway never introducing himself, his wife Hadley, nor formally explaining how or why they had come to Paris. The sadness of the opening paragraphs, the bad weather, the drunkards in the neighborhood, and the details of the collection of night soil establish a minor chord motif that will sound throughout the entire book, darkening happy chapters, keeping the tone pervasively ominous. The stormy weather in Paris also provides the bad weather in the story Hemingway is writing, apparently "The Three-Day Blow."

Hemingway casts himself as his artist-hero; this is his portrait of the artist as a young man. And as such, he portrays himself as hungry, hungry to create, hungry for experience, and—as an exiled artist—just plain poor and hungry. He denies himself comforts and distractions from his art, going hungry to sharpen his appetite for detail. At one point he complains to Sylvia Beach, owner of the rental library Shakespeare and Company. Then, afterward:

I was disgusted with myself for having complained about things. I was doing what I did of my own free will and I was doing it stupidly. I should have bought a large piece of bread and eaten it instead of skipping a meal. . . . You God damn complainer. You dirty phony saint and martyr, I said to myself. You quit journalism of your own accord. You have credit and Sylvia would have loaned you money. . . . And then the next thing you would be compromising on something else. Hunger is healthy and the pictures do look better when you are hungry. (p. 72)

The self-portrait as devoted artist is successful, and conforms wonderfully with stereotypes of those starving for their art in garrets, but it's a fiction: the Hemingways lived reasonably comfortably on Hadley's trust fund, augmented by what Ernest earned through occasional journalism and the sale of his poetry and fiction. The make-believe he would like the reader to credit is even undercut by the details Hemingway provides: he writes in a cheap hotel room so as not to be disturbed by Hadley; when it looks as if the fireplace in the hotel room will not draw and the room will be too cold to work in, he then moves to a café to write and fortifies himself with one coffee, two rum drinks, a dozen oysters, and a half liter of wine. The Hemingways can afford a cook in their two-room flat, to dine at Michaud's Restaurant, which was not cheap by French standards, as well as going on a winter excursion to Switzerland for the skiing, keeping the flat but giving up the hotel room for the duration. Hadley is complaisant in the extreme, worshipful and complimentary.

Like all his works, this book, too, is about aesthetics. Hemingway talks about his difficulty in writing one true sentence, presumably along the lines of the exercises Griffin and Baker print, but "true" for Hemingway obviously means not literally true, since he also talked about the truth of his fictional stories, but rather true-to-his-sense-of-life, mythically correct, with complete believability from the reader's perspective. He talks about learning from Cézanne's paintings on display at the Luxembourg Museum, and from Gertrude Stein about repetition of words and manipulating prose rhythms. But much of his description of Stein, as of others in the book, is demeaning. Stein likes artists, not their art, nor does she discuss their artistic experiments; she is very concerned about getting her work published—commercialism, not aestheticism—but she is lazy when it comes to revising her work, proofreading, or making her experimental prose intelligible. Stein, according to Hemingway, only praised those artists inferior to herself, which is ironic, since Hemingway in *A Moveable Feast* praises only those artists who are no threat to his reputation.

There are two major difficulties in dealing with *A Moveable Feast*. One, I have already discussed, is the problem of how much of the published text Hemingway himself would have released to the public. The second is separating the nasty and bitchy gossip from the marvelous prose that conveys it, a prose that returns to the early style without the sense of self-parody. There are wonderful evocations of places, people, and food, with no "reaching accurately and well." In the eighth chapter, "Hunger Is Good Discipline," the artist's attention to detail, gastronomic and otherwise, is apparent:

> The beer was very cold and wonderful to drink. The *pommes à l'huile* were firm and marinated and the olive oil delicious. I ground black pepper over the potatoes and moistened the bread in the olive oil. After the first heavy draft of beer I drank and ate very slowly. When the *pommes à l'huile* were gone I ordered another serving and a *cervelas*. This was a sausage like a heavy, wide frankfurter split in two and covered with a special mustard sauce. (pp. 72–73)

He eats these in Lipp's Brasserie, having received money for some creative writing, and he eats alone, yet persists in the starving-artist image. Where is Hadley while he is feasting at Lipp's (this is before their child is born; she is not babysitting), and, if they are indeed as poor as he wants readers to believe, what is she eating?

The chapter about Ford Madox Ford (the ninth) is critical of Ford throughout, his appearance, his bad breath, his mannerisms and pretensions, and his wheezing. Again, there's irony here, over and above the ungratefulness of Hemingway to someone who was helping him at the time. The chapter begins with Hemingway's describing those mutilated by the past war and his remark that he respected the mutilated more than those who might also be veterans but were not obviously mutilated; "In those days, we did not trust anyone who had not been in the war" (p. 82). Although Hemingway never tells the reader, Ford has indeed been in the war, volunteering in his early forties, when he was well beyond any draft, and his wheezing came from damage to his lungs by poison gas. In Hemingway's description, however, Ford comes off the fool, and Hemingway, the trusting, but observant naïf. Thus the critic, if he or she wishes to enjoy marvelously evocative prose, a wonderful celebration of Paris and the joys of being young, in love, and in Paris, and exquisitely rendered catty and bitchy portraits, must try to separate them from the insecure, ungracious artist who limned them.

"Birth of a New School," the tenth chapter, seems to have been added by Mary from Hemingway's manuscripts; it was not one of the stories submitted to Scribner's in 1959.[5] The thirteenth chapter, "A Strange Enough Ending," gives his version of his break with Gertrude Stein, presumably by overhearing a lover's quarrel between Gertrude and her live-in companion, Alice B. Toklas. That Gertrude and Alice were lesbians should not have come as a revelation, since they lived openly together, especially not after Stein had lectured Hemingway on the naturalness of lesbian love (chapter 2, "Miss Stein Instructs"). Nor does Hemingway condemn even by implication Sylvia Beach or Natalie Barney, both lesbians, the latter flagrantly and notoriously so. One can share his embarrassment at overhearing language not intended for others' ears, but it hardly seems enough to rupture a friendship.

The book contains portraits of Ezra Pound as extraordinarily kind and generous, and of minor poet Evan Shipman as not-too-proud to help a waiter with his garden. Penultimately, there is a three-chapter portrait of F. Scott Fitzger-

ald that portrays him as an alcoholic who prostitutes his
writing skill and behaves badly, childishly, when drunk, and
that portrays Zelda Fitzgerald, Scott's wife, as jealous of his
work and insane. Again, these chapters are fictionally true:
they are based on fact, and elements have been corrobo-
rated by others, but whether the details are, in fact, what
actually happened or not,[6] the picture that emerges is one
with the rest of the book. Young Hemingway is an artist
concerned with aesthetics, loyalty, and the self-control and
discipline needed to create great art, and Stein, Ford, and
Fitzgerald are not. Nevertheless, Hemingway can say of
Scott:

His talent was as natural as the pattern that was made by the dust
on a butterfly's wings. At one time he understood it no more than
the butterfly did and he did not know when it was brushed or
marred. Later he became conscious of his damaged wings and of
their construction and he learned to think and could not fly any-
more because the love of flight was gone and he could only remember when it had been effortless.   (p. 147)

The last chapter, the twentieth, is titled "There Is Never
Any End to Paris." Along with the preface, where Hemingway wrestled in manuscript with apologies to his first two
wives and with the question of the fictionality of the work,
the last chapter is the most rewritten part of the manuscript. It deals, along with the winter skiing at Schruns,
Austria, with the breakup of his marriage to Hadley
through his affair with second-wife-to-be, Pauline. Incredibly, Hemingway blames his own misconduct on being se-
duced, not only by Pauline (who is never named), but by a
close friend who introduced him to the rich, thus corrupt-
ing him and spoiling him as starving and dedicated artist.
(The friend is John Dos Passos, the rich are Gerald and
Sara Murphy, and none are named.) "All things truly
wicked start from an innocence. . . . You lie and hate it and
it destroys you and every day is more dangerous, but you
live day by day as in a war" (p. 210). It is almost as if Hemingway were casting himself in the role of the young bull-

fighter, Romero, corrupted by the "jet-setting" expatriates. But Hemingway at twenty-six was no nineteen-year-old Pedro Romero: Hemingway had covered the police beat for the *Kansas City Star*, gone to war, covered the news of Europe for the *Toronto Star*. The fictional young author in *A Moveable Feast* may be a naïf, but Hemingway was not, and these last pages ring of excuse and special pleading that mar the believable tone to that point. The book then concludes on an elegiac note that the minor chords of sadness throughout the book had prepared the reader for:

That was the end of the first part of Paris. . . .
There is never any ending to Paris and the memory of each person who has lived in it differs from that of any other. . . . Paris was always worth it and you received return for whatever you brought to it. But this is how Paris was in the early days when we were poor and happy. (p. 211)

Two years previous, Gene Z. Hanrahan had published *The Wild Years* (New York: Dell, 1962), seventy-three journalistic pieces Hemingway had done for the Toronto *Star*s *(Daily* and *Weekly)* in the early twenties. These collections of early Hemingway materials proliferated in the posthumous years. Matthew Bruccoli published Hemingway's journalism for the Kansas City *Star* and his high school writings in *Tabula* and *The Trapeze* (1970 and 1971), and William White published first a selection of his journalism from 1920 through 1956 in *By-Line: Ernest Hemingway* (1967), then the complete Toronto *Star* articles in *Dateline: Toronto* (1985). In 1979 Nicholas Gerogiannis published and annotated eighty-eight poems of Hemingway's that he could locate, mostly very bad poems, *Ernest Hemingway/ Complete Poems*. And in 1972, Scribner's, with the help of Professor Philip Young, published *The Nick Adams Stories*, all of Hemingway's stories that involved Nick Adams, including at-that-time unpublished fragments, or sections cut from previously published stories; Young wrote an introduction and tried to arrange the stories chronologically as they would be in Nick's lifetime, arousing some critical controversy over his arrangement.[7]

After World War II, Hemingway had spoken of a great land, air, and sea novel, and biographers assume that he was contemplating a three-part war novel incorporating his experiences as a correspondent covering the war from the air with the RAF, on land with the U.S. 4th Infantry Division in France and Luxembourg, and on the water hunting submarines from the *Pilar*. Of this projected trilogy, only the sea part, *Islands in the Stream,* ever got written. Hemingway began the book in 1946, at about the same time he began *Garden of Eden,* writing most of the first, or Bimini section, putting it aside in April 1947 when Patrick was seriously ill after an auto accident. He took it up late in 1950, writing the Cuba section. Then he switched his energies to *The Old Man and the Sea,* repeating in that story the fight to land a fish he had already rehearsed in the Bimini section of *Islands.* Then in the spring of 1951 he wrote the last section of the novel. *Islands in the Stream* was also envisioned as a trilogy, sometimes called "The Sea When Young," "The Sea When Absent," and "The Sea in Being." *The Old Man and the Sea* constituted an awkward fourth part that did not fit the other three, having the same locale as the last two parts—Cuba—but no shared characters. Hemingway wisely separated *The Old Man and the Sea* and published it by itself, continuing to work on *Islands* throughout 1951, then abandoning the manuscript in a bank vault in Cuba, where Mary recovered it in 1961. She and Charles Scribner, Jr., edited the unfinished manuscript, pared down redundancies, eliminated uncompleted plot lines—

Beyond the routine chores of correcting spelling and punctuation, we made some cuts in the manuscript, I feeling that Ernest would surely have made them himself. The book is all Ernest's. We have added nothing to it.[8]

What Mary did add were the titles. Ernest had applied "The Island and the Stream" to the first section of the book, the Bimini or "The Sea When Young" section. Mary titled the sections less pretentiously "Bimini," "Cuba," and "At Sea," and, since Bimini and Cuba were both islands, titled the whole *Islands in the Stream,* suggesting both the geographical islands and the Gulf Stream, and little man in the historical stream of time.

Islands in the Stream, as we have it, is the third-person story of a painter named Thomas Hudson (named for an explorer and another very large stream). Hudson lives off inherited oil money and thus can paint as he wishes. He has a ranch in Montana, a house in Bimini, and another house in Cuba. His history is remarkably like Hemingway's, growing up in Ojibwa country, spending his young manhood in Paris with Joyce, Pound, Ford, and painter Jules Pascin, then living in Cuba. Hudson, when the novel opens, has been twice married, has three sons, and a writer friend and alter ego, Roger Davis, who also was in Paris with Joyce and Pound. (Hemingway at one time considered Roger as the protagonist. Like Hemingway, Roger is a writer, he calls women, even those he is sleeping with, "daughter," and the boys in this version are his sons; there is a published fragment concerning a drive by Roger across the country titled "The Strange Country" that concludes *The Complete Short Stories of Ernest Hemingway.*)

"Bimini" concerns Hudson's house on Bimini—although the island is named only in the section heading—Hudson's art, his friendship with Roger, his insomnia, and the arrival and entertainment of his three sons for five weeks. Many of the reminiscences between the father and young Tom, the oldest son, are about Paris and sound like *A Moveable Feast,* which was written afterward but published first. Two significant episodes include the middle son, David. In one, he is spearfishing and pursued by a hammerhead shark. Thomas tries to kill the shark with a rifle and misses, and the boat's alcoholic mate and cook kills it with a tommy gun. Later, David, about thirteen years old, fights for six hours to land a broadbill swordfish, only to lose it at the very end. Here, the echoes are, of course, of *The Old Man and the Sea,* and the moral is the same: courage and skill are not always enough to win. Like Santiago, David identifies with the fish he is trying to catch—"Then I began to love him more than anything on earth" (p. 142).[9] The boys

leave, and shortly after, Hudson receives word that the two
younger sons have been killed in an auto accident with their
mother (possibly suggested by the auto accident in which
Patrick and Gregory were injured). David has lost his fish
and borne up well; Hudson has lost two sons and must
now do the same.

In the "Cuba" section, Hudson has returned from the sea
to his house. Hemingway's technique of omission is annoy-
ing here. Hudson is remarried and getting letters from the
South Pacific from his third wife, whom we never see. She
is presumably a correspondent, like Hemingway's own third
wife Martha Gellhorn, but nothing is explained: not the
marriage, nor the separation, nor their obvious antipathy.
Similarly, Hudson's sea-time activities are based on Hemingway's Q-boat adventures on the *Pilar*, but this is also not
explained. The reader is only given enough to believe that
Hudson has been on dangerous missions at sea. What is
made explicit is that Hudson's eldest son, young Tom, has
enlisted in the RAF and has been shot down and killed over
France.

The middle section is the weakest of a weak book. It is
almost entirely windy conversation: Hudson with Boise, the
cat he loves, with the inhabitants of the Floridita Bar in Havana, and finally with his movie-actress first wife, an imi-
tation Marlene Dietrich, briefly back in Cuba for the USO
and for brief lovemaking with Hudson, and then another
argument. The conversation Hemingway records is garrulous, reminiscent of *Across the River and into the Trees*.
Hemingway better conveys Hudson's abilities to absorb dai-
quiris than his grief or his continuing passion for his first
wife. The reader is told that she is an actress, but nothing
was said about her acting during the Paris years when Hudson was studying art there. Moreover, most of Hudson's
Paris friends are writers, the writers of *A Moveable Feast*,
not painters. Although the reader is told that Hudson
paints—and finishes paintings very quickly—I am no more
convinced that Hudson is a painter than I am that Frederic
Henry was a student of architecture. The scenery that Hemingway provides is lush and detailed, but the eye that de-

scribes it is that of an observant novelist or hunter, not a painter. At one point, Hudson is recounting a stay in Hong Kong and the gift of three beautiful young prostitutes for an evening (an anecdote Hemingway also told about himself).[10] "I looked at them all asleep and I wished I could take a picture of them" (p. 295). One has to wonder why an accomplished artist, a skilled realist painter, if he wants a reminder of the occasion, laments the absence of a camera and doesn't sketch them. Hudson is very close to Ernest Hemingway. His memories are memories readers have encountered elsewhere in Hemingway's work, without much change. And the uses made of those memories, artistically or philosophically, are neither new nor terribly engaging.

The third section of the novel, "At Sea," recounts the pursuit by Hudson and his crew of German submariners. Presumably, Hudson and his men sighted a sub and called in an air strike on it. The sub escaped, though damaged, and had to be abandoned. The German crew attack a small key in the chain of islands, swamps, and mangrove thickets off the north coast of Cuba, massacring the inhabitants and stealing their boats. Hudson sails after them in his unnamed boat, but externally very much like the *Pilar,* trying to anticipate their course, cut them off, and capture at least one prisoner. His sons are dead, he has stopped painting for the duration of the war, it appears, and his pursuit seems the embodiment of a death wish that is realized. Standing on the bridge of his boat in a narrow channel, expecting attack, Hudson is ambushed and shot three times. His crew kill the Germans, but at novel's end, the reader is led to believe that Hudson's wounds are fatal.

Parts of *Islands in the Stream* are exciting, and parts reiterate Hemingway's philosophy: that a man's choices and actions define him, and that craftsmanship is very important. But there is nothing new. Characters are neither well developed nor integrated. Roger Davis and the woman he leaves Bimini with are never mentioned again. Hudson's crew is somewhat individualized, but the characters never come alive on their own; they are never given pasts nor reasons for being with Hudson, and thus remain foils to him, characters known by their quirks or abilities, but not as people. Overall, the novel is talky, deserving of more pruning by Charles Scribner and Mary; and, if they could not tie the whole together more tightly, integrate the characters and their relationships, developing the significances of the various actions, then it would have been better to have published the self-contained excerpts—David's adventures with shark and broadbill, Hudson's hunt—rather than the incomplete novel. It adds no luster to Hemingway's reputation; to the contrary, it makes him seem unable to control his verboseness or to write with a sure, well-developed artistic plan in mind.

In 1985 Scribner's reissued *The Dangerous Summer* in book form, collecting the three *Life* magazine pieces from 1960 that described the bullfighting duel of Antonio Ordóñez and Luis Miguel Dominguín, reediting them, and presenting them with an introduction by James Michener and a different selection of photographs. There was no particular reason to have Michener introduce the volume, other than, perhaps, to help guarantee its sales by adding Michener's fans to those of Hemingway's. Michener tells of a tenuous connection in his introduction: he had been asked by *Life* in 1952 to read *The Old Man and the Sea* before *Life* took the chance to publish it as a single issue; its success prompted *Life* to repeat the novella-in-a-single-issue, and Michener was next with his *The Bridges of Toko-ri,* the following June. Michener had met Hemingway only once, and at that time displayed his own ample knowledge of bullfighting to Hemingway. His introduction is chatty and pleasant and runs to thirty-seven pages, most of the last twenty being a glossary on bullfighting, redundant because Scribner's has added Hemingway's own glossary from *Death in the Afternoon* to the end of the book. Michener's comment on the original, uncut manuscript, before Hotchner and Hemingway edited it (he saw only part 2), is that it was unpublishable: "redundant, wandering in parts, and burdened with bullfighting minutiae."[11]

As Michener acknowledges regarding the Scribner's edition (pp. 37–38), "the purely bullfight passages have been sharply cut. . . . [And the editor decided] to eliminate from most of the corridas the names and works of matadors other than Dominguín and Ordóñez." Surely "the purely bullfight passages" is a phrase that is pure Hemingway. There is, however, much remaining that is about bullfights. It amazed me, now having read the bullfight descriptions in *The Sun Also Rises, Death in the Afternoon,* and *The Dangerous Summer* in close succession, how Hemingway, using a vocabulary of descriptors largely limited to *controlled, good, true, slowly, emotional, beautiful, close, smoothly,* and *suavely,* is able to picture bullfight after bullfight without ever exactly repeating himself. And there are magical descriptive passages, such as this one:

[We saw] where two storks were nesting on the roof of a house. . . . The nest was half built, the female had not laid her eggs yet and they were courting. The male would stroke her neck with his bill and she would look up at him with storklike devotion and then look away and he would stroke her again. (p. 67)

Although most of the garrulousness has been pruned by editors, what remains is the attitude that produced it: that every word Hemingway utters is important; that he is important, a necessary part of the bullfighter's entourage, for morale and an accurate assessment of the day's fighting. He even assumes that the bullfighter kills the bull in a certain manner "to please me" (p. 58). The same egotism is evinced in his cavalier manner toward Mary, who suffers colds, a broken toe, and jealousy from attractive American tourists whom Ernest picks up, but who is usually mentioned only as someone needing to be cared for, rarely as an appreciative and knowing spectator at the corridas.

The editing of the manuscript also is problematical. Certain things that appeared in *Life* are not here; passages appear here that were not in *Life.* That's to be expected. But certain sentences appear in both versions, but with differences in them. As in *A Moveable Feast,* it appears as if someone is changing the author's words. A dangling modifier is silently corrected, the phrase "safer than" is changed

to "as safe as" and "Some unscrupulous managers" becomes the more-inclusive "The unscrupulous managers."[12]
The Spanish adjective form *Manchego* is Anglicized to
Manchegan and *Las Campanas* becomes *Campanas*. Two
guests are mentioned on page 87, but the editing has eliminated their identities. Whose words are these? At Málaga,
Hemingway describes the fight in detail, saying that each of
the bulls has been killed with only a single thrust of the
sword, but with the first bull, "the sword slid in sideways
and the point showed out through the hide behind the
bull's shoulders. A banderillero pulled the sword out with
a swing of his cape and Luis Miguel killed the bull with the
descabello" (p. 169), which Hemingway defines as killing
"the bull . . . by driving the point of the sword between the
base of the skull and the first vertebra" (p. 211), but obviously, by a second sword thrust. If the editors are correcting inconsistencies, why not this one, not apparent in the
Life account since the killing of the first two bulls was
omitted? The editing raises many questions, even down to
the incomplete index.

   The Dangerous Summer is not a great book. For those
who have not read *Death in the Afternoon,* it conveys
something of Hemingway's passion for the sport, but it
does not convey the aesthetic concerns to the same degree.
Hemingway rails against the shaved horns of bulls and
against the circus tricks that he thinks spoil the art of bullfighting, and he makes one specific statement linking the
art of bullfighting to art in general:

A bullfighter can never see the work of art that he is making. He
has no chance to correct it as a painter or a writer has. He cannot
hear it as a musician can. He can only feel it and hear the crowd's
reaction to it. When he feels it and knows that it is great it takes
hold of him so that nothing else in the world matters.   (p. 198)

But the book is not cohesive, even less so than *A Moveable
Feast,* and it is not entirely Hemingway's: to a certain extent, it is A. E. Hotchner's, James Michener's, and the editors of Scribner's.

The same thing is true of the following book from Scribner's, Hemingway's *The Garden of Eden* (1986). Hemingway had begun the novel after World War II in 1946, and by 1947 there were 100 pages typed and 900 in longhand. Ultimately there were 1,500 pages to the novel, unfinished in Hemingway's lifetime. Charles Scribner, Jr., tried to edit the text but felt too respectful of its author to edit ruthlessly, and so hired an outside editor, Tom Jenks, to put the manuscript into publishable form. Jenks cut some two-thirds of the manuscript, at least three major characters, and two major images that control much of the novel. In the manuscript, there are two young couples, a painter and his wife, Nick and Barbara Sheldon, who live in Paris in a flat much like that of Hadley and Ernest Hemingway, and a young writer and his wife, David and Catherine Bourne. The four have a writer friend, Andy Murray. In the manuscript, the Bournes and the Sheldons visit the Rodin Museum in Paris, see Rodin's statue *The Metamorphoses of Ovid* of two women embracing, one reclining, the other kneeling. The statue is a variant of two women embracing that Rodin had done for the top right corner of his *Gates of Hell;* there they are identified as "The Damned Women." Barbara conceives a lesbian passion for Catherine that is never consummated; she does sleep with Andy on the same day that Nick is killed in a road accident, and in guilt and remorse, Barbara commits suicide. All of these plot lines have been cut from the published novel, along with the statue *The Metamorphoses,* which is the key to the multiple instances of, and references to, change.

The other basic image omitted occurs during a visit to the Prado Museum in Madrid, where Hieronymus Bosch's *Garden of Earthly Delights,* a triptych, is displayed. *The Garden of Earthly Delights* applies to the central panel of the painting, where fruits and sexual pleasures of wide variety are being tasted; the left-hand panel is a chaste Edenic scene, the right-hand panel one of hellish torments. Bosch's *Garden,* as well as that of Genesis, would seem to be the source of the novel's title, but this art work, too, has been cut.

What is left in the published novel is some five months of
the honeymoon and breakup of the marriage of David and
Catherine. The initial days are idyllic, and then Catherine is
beset both by irrationality that manifests itself in jealousy
of David's work and a desire to be a dominant male herself,
a desire that leads briefly to sexual inversion. She picks up
a lovely lesbian, Marita, and brings her back to the hotel at
which she and David are staying on the Riviera. The mé-
nage à trois is intensified because she expects to share Marita sexually with David. Soon David falls in love with both
women, echoing Hemingway's situation of being married to
Hadley and loving both her and Pauline. The honeymoon
of David and Catherine takes place in Le Grau-du-Roi,
France, where Hemingway and Pauline honeymooned. The
name Catherine, of course, occurs in *A Farewell to Arms,*
and Nick was often an alter ego for Hemingway in *The
Nick Adams Stories.* One has the sense in reading of en-
countering old friends, especially since the Riviera setting
and activities of the characters are reminiscent of Fitzgerald's *Tender Is the Night* (which also included Gerald and
Sara Murphy), and of Zelda Fitzgerald's jealousy of Scott's
work and her insanity. Hemingway seems to have blended
in fact and fiction about his first two wives and his fourth
(although Martha may have lent some of her name to Marita), along with Zelda and Scott Fitzgerald, and himself.

The publication of the novel was greeted with much interest for its sexual content and its supposed revelation of a
gentler, less macho, more androgynous Hemingway. The
prurient fascination was heightened by Kenneth S. Lynn's
biography (*Hemingway,* New York: Simon and Schuster,
1987), which insisted that Hemingway had been sexually
confused by his mother who had kept him in dresses and
long hair until he went to school and who had raised him
as a twin of his sister Marcelline. There is little new sexually in *The Garden of Eden.* Lesbianism occurs in such
short stories as "Mr. and Mrs. Elliot" (1925) and "A Sea
Change" (1931; "a sea change," from *The Tempest* and
The Waste Land, anticipates the theme of metamorphosis

in *The Garden of Eden*); in *For Whom the Bell Tolls,* Pilar
admits her attraction to Maria. The desire to look like another, dress like another, wear one's hair like another runs
through Hemingway's fiction: Brett Ashley wears short hair
and men's hats; Catherine Barkley wants Frederic Henry to
let his hair "grow a little longer and I could cut mine and
we'd be just alike only one of us blonde and one of us
dark" (*A Farewell to Arms,* p. 299). Maria has close-
cropped hair growing from her shaved head and feels that
"neither one can tell that one of us is one and not the
other. . . . I would be thee because I love thee so" (*For
Whom the Bell Tolls,* pp. 262–63). Catherine Bourne cuts
her hair short to be exactly like her husband's, then after
dying it, persuades David to have his dyed the same. They
wear identical clothing, shorts, and fishermen's shirts,
shorts on a woman in France in the twenties being scandal-
ous. Hemingway was undoubtedly a hair fetishist, but for a
lover to desire to be one with the beloved, to achieve one-
ness and identity is universal and hardly a perversion. And
although Hemingway is maddeningly discreet in describing
the sexual practices in *The Garden of Eden,* one of Catherine's "devil" practices seems to be assuming the superior
position over David. That seems not devilish, nor androgynous, nor a symptom of forthcoming lesbianism.

Catherine tans herself to a very dark shade, the darkness
explicitly foreshadowing her mental darkness. Then she
bleaches her hair, contrasting the dark and the light, and
persuades David to do the same. David furthers these images of contrast by staring at his face in the mirror shaved
only on one side (pp. 167–68), images also of ambivalence:
male/female; creative/sterile, David as author, Catherine unable to conceive (p. 71); love/hate, David loves Catherine
but is repulsed by her madness and does hate her for burn-
ing his manuscripts; for David, Catherine/Marita, for
Catherine, David/Marita; Marita says she loves them both
(p. 98). But Hemingway had explored ambivalences before.
He examined the killing of men and animals throughout his
work, in terms of the morality involved. Sexually, he exam-

ined the shifting roles of men and women and their ambiv-
alent desires. Brett is the new twenties woman. She refuses
to accept outmoded definitions of feminine propriety. She
dresses as she pleases, drinks like a man, sleeps around like
a man, yet nurtures injured males as females traditionally
have. Frederic Henry is something of a soldier, however unsuccessful, yet he nurtures swagger-stick-wielding Catherine, nurses her (even donning a gown to do so). Maria is a
traditionally subservient woman, but Pilar is the leader of a
guerrilla band, even if her military scepter is the stew pot
spoon. *The Garden of Eden* only makes more explicit this
examination of sexual roles and sexual ambiguities within
everyone. What the surprised critics seem to have forgotten
is that Hemingway had been depicting women for decades
(whether successfully or not) and that as author he had to
make an emotional identification with them in order to de-
pict them; all authors do. Now he continues that identification, continuing to examine feminine traits within his
male protagonist and male characteristics in his female
characters.

Initially David is happy with his new wife on their honeymoon, but the discontents rapidly accumulate. They move
frequently in the five months the published novel covers,
from Le-Grau-du-Roi in May to La Naupole to Hendaye to
Madrid, back to La Naupole where the novel ends in September. At first David doesn't write, spending time with
Catherine. Her first jealousy comes when David's publisher
sends him clippings of reviews of his second novel. Later
David begins a narrative of their honeymoon, and Catherine is pleased: the narrative will give her permanence in
literature, capture the early joy of their now-strained marriage. She envisions it illustrated by Picasso, Pascin (whom
Scribner's misspells as Pascen), André Derain, Raoul Dufy,
and Marie Laurencin. Then David interrupts writing that
novel to write stories of East Africa, where he grew up, stories about his brutal father, and Catherine resents the aban-
donment of their narrative. Again, David is pulled in
different directions between the two writing projects, as he
is between Catherine and Marita. He asserts his indepen-

dence by abandoning the novel, turning to the African stories. Incensed, Catherine burns the stories. Although David,
in the published version, says he abandoned the marriage
narrative, that story is obviously what we are reading, in
The Garden of Eden, making the novel one of those convo-
luted reflexive novels about an author writing a novel, and
a very rare third-person example of that genre.

In The Garden of Eden, Hemingway's concerns are not
just psychological, but aesthetic, as usual, particularly as he
enters David's consciousness as he writes. Since David is
very much like Hemingway and writes very much like
Hemingway, the disclosures are very interesting.

and when the sun rose out of the sea [at La Naupole] it had, for
him, risen long before and he was well into the crossing of the
gray, dried, bitter lakes, his boots now white with crusted alka-
lis. (p. 138)

The "he" here is David's father, and Hemingway shows
David identifying with his character. Technique is also a
matter of concern:

he had been trying to remember truly how he felt and what had
happened on that day. The hardest to make truly was how he had
felt and keep it untinctured by how he had felt later. (p. 174)

Another passage echoes the opening remarks on writing
from Death in the Afternoon: "he must not show it by ar-
bitrary statements of rhetoric but by remembering the actual things that had brought it" (p. 182).

After Catherine burns the African stories and leaves,
David is briefly unable to write. Since the African stories
are based on Hemingway's trip to Africa in 1953–54, they
have to have been added to the manuscript in that decade.
After the plane crashes, Hemingway's physical and mental
problems increased. By 1960, writing had become extremely difficult. Barbara Probst Solomon suggests that the
following sentence, describing David's efforts, are actually
a description of Hemingway's own difficulties during this
late period:[13]

He had started a sentence as soon as he had gone into his working room and had completed it but he could write nothing after
it. He crossed it out and started another sentence and again came
to the complete blankness. He was unable to write the sentence
that should follow although he knew it. He wrote a first simple
declarative sentence again and it was impossible for him to put
down the next sentence on paper. At the end of two hours it was
the same.   (p. 239)

But lovemaking with warm, understanding, supportive
Marita miraculously cures him, and the next day, in the
published text, he is able to remember one of the African
stories completely and rewrite it better than before. The
novel ends with David, his craft intact, united to Marita,
whose name is very close to *marital*, in English, French, or
Italian. Marita is one of those women whom early Hemingway critics derided as too good to be true: beautiful, rich,
multilingual, more womanly than Catherine (by her own
claim, p. 192), a better wife (Catherine says of Marita,
"That's being a good wife" [p. 109]), and understanding of
David's work, which she has read even before they meet,
and is not threatened by it, as Catherine is. She easily and
incredibly switches from lesbianism to presumably faithful
heterosexuality. Her role, David's easy switching from
Catherine to her, and his equally easy ability to remember
and rewrite his stories are the hardest things to believe in
the novel.

The easiest is the one long African story that Hemingway
shares with us, an initiation tale, like Faulkner's "The
Bear." David as a boy discovers a hugely tusked bull elephant by moonlight and tells his father and his father's native friend Juma about it. The three track the elephant for
several days, David thereby proving his endurance and wor-
thiness to be a hunter, but simultaneously identifying with
the elephant, wishing that his father and Juma would not
kill it. They track it to the skeleton of another elephant
Juma killed five years before, when he had also wounded
the bull they are tracking. David is increasingly remorseful
for having betrayed the bull to his father and Juma. He con-

trasts their greed for the bull's ivory tusks and their drunken, destructive lives to the tenderness shown by the bull to his dead comrade. And his maturation is simultaneously a loss of innocence and a separation from his father, just as the adult David's maturation comes with his remorseful separation from the garden of innocence and from his tempting Eve, Catherine. David calls her bleached hair ivory, insisting on the connection.

Like all the works considered in this chapter, *The Garden of Eden* was unfinished and not ready for publication. What Scribner's and the author's heirs have given the public is a truncated version with one of the main stories but most of the artistic connective tissue missing. Had they been genuinely interested in preserving Hemingway's reputation as a major author, I think it would have been better to have published just the elephant story along with, as an appendix, David's comments on writing. Hemingway's journals of the African trips in the midfifties still remain unpublished, excerpts only appearing in two parts in *Look* magazine (see note 4, the previous chapter, p. 143) and in *Sports Illustrated,* 20 Dec. 71, 41–70; 3 Jan. 72, 26–46; 10 Jan. 72, 22–50. If they are also in unfinished form, display the same tedious garrulousness that the second part displayed, and reveal nothing more about Hemingway and his art than is already known, then it would be better for Hemingway's reputation that they not be published, lest readers seem like David's father and Juma, jackals enriching themselves on the corpse of a giant.

7

Hemingway's Importance

It should be obvious by now that my feelings for Hemingway the man are not the same as my feelings for his fiction, and that even within the fiction my respect varies. His works are uneven, and he could be unkind, ungrateful, and a boastful bully. The psychobiographical works being done about him have the fascination of titillating gossip, but they tend to focus on the man and reveal little new about the work, and it is because of his writing that Hemingway is important, one of the major American writers of the twentieth century, and of the world.

Hemingway was not the only writer of his era to insist on realism—Fitzgerald, Faulkner, and Dos Passos were among many others. But Hemingway was extremely influential because he was not just a respected writer but also a popular one. His simple style was easy to read, and its inclusions of sex and violence made it attractive to the general audience. (Fitzgerald's first novel, the ungainly, romantic *This Side of Paradise*, was his most popular; his later, better-written novels did not sell as well. Faulkner was almost out of print in this country before Malcolm Cowley rescued him with a portable edition in 1946.) Thus the accessibility of Hemingway's prose, plus his frequently exciting subject matter, along with his exciting life-style, made him extremely influential.

Before Hemingway, many writers of war tried to give "the big picture." The position of regiments and brigades, the movement of troops and lines of battle, and most readers were confused. Since Hemingway (who followed Stephen Crane in *The Red Badge of Courage*), most writers of war leave placement and movement of regiments to historians and concentrate instead on the actions and feelings of individuals in battle.

His pessimistic writings in the twenties were a healthy corrective to the optimism of late Victorianism and American Progressivism. If World War I did not convince all that the attitude associated with Pollyanna was wrong, then the Depression and World War II certainly did. Twenty years before Jean-Paul Sartre and Albert Camus, Hemingway was writing existentialism: there are no a priori values; people create their values by their choices and actions, defining themselves in the process. This point of view replaced cheerful optimism as the dominant literary philosophy, and is, together with the realism that Hemingway also secured, still with us. Modern readers distrust unbelievable happy endings; they distrust those coincidences that make everything work out all right. But Hemingway was not a systematic philosopher, and he is most valued, not for what he said, but for how he said it, his style.

He explored, like James Joyce and Sherwood Anderson before him, little incidents of life that gave both the character in his fiction and the reader outside it insight into life. Frequently the incidents were not as dramatic as the deflowering of Liz Coates in "Up in Michigan" or the wounding of Nick Adams in chapter 6 of *In Our Time,* but rather mundane events like the domestic dispute in "The Doctor and the Doctor's Wife" or a fishing trip such as in "Big Two-Hearted River." Hemingway had a natural talent as a storyteller, one well capable of holding the reader's interest, and he developed the ability to find symbols within the indigeneous landscape of the story that communicated beyond the superficial level of the events within the story. As a journalist, he was able to convey a sense of daily life and link the action of his stories and novels to events in the larger world beyond them. For all these reasons, Hemingway is important, but preeminently he is remembered for the way he wrote.

I have already discussed his style in chapter 2, but let me briefly restate a description of the prose. For a variety of

reasons—distrust of official rhetoric, whether his parents'
or the government's, journalistic training, and personal pre-
dilection—Hemingway's initial prose featured simple, declarative sentences that avoided abstract terms and editorial
judgments. Instead, the prose focused on concrete objects,
the sights, words, and objects that were poetically linked to
emotion. The author guided the reader's judgments by these
words, actions, and objects, but rarely told the reader what
or how to think (and when the words were ironic, sometimes confused the reader inattentive to tone). The first-
person narrator told readers about his own feelings, rarely
speculating about another's. Thus, in accordance with modernist principles, the reader had to make judgments, had to
make the connections, emotional, psychological, and moral
in this connect-the-dot artwork presented by the author.

The simple, declarative sentences, thus, were emotionally
and artistically compressed, bearing much weight for their
seeming simplicity. They constituted a prose poem, insisting
on interpretation by their audience, the reader. This delighted many critics, earning Hemingway a reputation
among them, without losing less-sophisticated readers, who
had difficulty with the long, complex, highly modified, pe-
riodic sentences of Henry James's later style or even the
less-convoluted prose of William Dean Howells. As the
pace of the century increased, as cars, planes, radios, and
telephones quickened the rate at which things were done,
the short, sometimes staccato sentences of Hemingway
seemed more in line with the times than the leisurely prose
constructions of his predecessors. Certainly the harsh world
he described was more familiar to them than the elegant
drawing rooms of James's.

Hemingway's prose is also effective because of the way
that the style seems to express the content. It is a bare-
bones prose embodying an existentialist, unoptimistic philosophy. There are few causative connectors, few *therefores*
or *becauses*. Hemingway's most frequent connector is *and*,
linking things temporally, not logically. "This happened
and then this happened." The world is absurd, misfortune
occurs, and patterns of causality are often inventions of a

mind desperately seeking order, projections, not demonstrable fact. The realist author then simply records what happened and leaves conclusions to the reader, although he has provided intense clues about the characters' deep emotional involvement with the events described.

Few students of creative writing avoid going through a Hemingway phase, a period of describing hard-luck men and women in stripped-down, highly suggestive prose. Writers as diverse as Norman Mailer, Tom Stoppard, and Raymond Carver have acknowledged Hemingway's influence upon them. The sentence structure taught in schools now, without elaborate modification, without carefully balanced clauses, but with an emphasis on clarity, concision, and illustrative detail is much closer to Hemingway than it is to Henry James or even Mark Twain in his third-person descriptive passages. Hemingway changed the way writers of English in the twentieth century used the language. He has many good stories and they will last, but his greatest accomplishment was with language.

Notes

Chapter 1: A Crowded Life

1. See Michael Reynolds, *The Young Hemingway* (London: Basil Blackwell, 1986), pp. 70–71, 77–87; also Reynolds's "Hemingway's Home: Depression and Suicide," *American Literature* 57 (December 1985): pp. 600–610.
2. Examples of these stories may be seen, in their entirety, in Peter Griffin's *Along with Youth* (New York: Oxford University Press, 1985), pp. 104–12, 174–80, 200–209.
3. Carlos Baker, *Ernest Hemingway: A Life Story* (New York: Scribner's, 1969), pp. 90–91, reprints some of these.
4. Quoted by Arthur Krock, a panelist for the Pulitzer Prize selection, in his column "In the Nation" for the New York *Times,* May 11, 1962, p. 30.
5. Jacqueline Tavernier-Courbin doubts that the blue notebooks were ever lost, stored at the Ritz, and belatedly recovered. She believes that Hemingway made the announcement, taken up by the press, as a way of preparing an audience for *A Moveable Feast* ("The Manuscripts of *A Moveable Feast, Hemingway notes* 6 [Spring 1981]: pp. 9–10).
6. Hemingway had written of suicide as early as his high-school story "The Judgment of Manitou," and again in *In Our Time*'s "Indian Camp" and *For Whom the Bell Tolls.* But a passage in *Death in the Afternoon* probably sums up his thoughts on the matter, governing his own suicide. He is describing the lingering and painful death of the bullfighter Gitanillo from a goring that led to spinal meningitis, repeated ruptures of the femoral artery, and a final loss of half his bodily weight:

It seemed a crime to keep him alive and he would have been much luckier to have died soon after the fight while he still

had control of himself and still possessed his courage rather
than to have gone through the progressive horror of physical
and spiritual humiliation that the long enough continued
bearing of unbearable pain produces   (p. 220).

Chapter 2: Creation of a New Prose

1. Ezra Pound, "A Retrospect," *Literary Essays of Ezra Pound*,
   ed. T. S. Eliot (London: Faber and Faber, 1954), pp. 4–5.
2. An introductory passage to "Indian Camp" was deleted by
   Hemingway and not published in *In Our Time*, nor in the
   Transatlantic Review (April 1924), where the story was first
   published. This introduction has been published as "Three
   Shots" in *The Nick Adams Stories*.
3. *Writers at Work: The "Paris Review" Interviews: Second Series*, ed. George Plimpton (New York: Viking Press, 1963), p.
   235. See also Hemingway's *Death in the Afternoon*, p. 192,
   for the first published expression of the "iceberg" theory, and
   A Moveable Feast, pp. 75, 76, for a later one. The passage
   quoted from *The Paris Review* is the most succinct.
4. As with "Indian Camp," Hemingway wrote more to the story
   than was originally published. A long conclusion, "On Writing," has also been published in *The Nick Adams Stories*.
5. William Balassi, "The Trail to *The Sun Also Rises*: The First
   Seven Days of Writing," The Third International Hemingway
   Conference, Schruns, Austria, June 22, 1988, p. 1.
6. Hemingway may have been furthered in his purpose by his
   recent reading of Sherwood Anderson, who also discusses social (not sexual) impotence in *Dark Laughter* (New York:
   Boni & Liveright, 1925):

   Have you noticed . . . that all of the people you see are tired
   out, impotent? . . . And if this war isn't a sign of universal
   impotence, sweeping over the world like a disease, then I
   don't know much.   (p. 42)

7. *The Waste Land* is T. S. Eliot's epochal poem of 1922 which
   condemned the lack of spiritual values in the corrupt, com-
   mercialized, lustful postwar world of the 1920s, urging instead the virtues of giving, sympathy, and control.
   Fragmented in form, allusive in nature, the poem lacks any
   obvious central narrative core, but references are made to a

number of religions and anthropological religious rites that contrast with the spiritual infertility, the waste land qualities, of the present. Eliot also alludes to a variety of literary figures from Dante, the Bible, Shakespeare's *The Tempest,* Ovid's *Metamorphoses,* and, among others, medieval romances of the Grail quest, in which the sexually wounded Fisher King, guardian of the Grail, awaits the worthy, questing knight to heal him and his barren land.

8. In addition to borrowing wasteland imagery, Jake-as-Fisher King, and a spiritual quest from T. S. Eliot's *The Waste Land,* Hemingway may also have been reinforced in his emphasis on the need for control by Eliot's use of *damyata,* at the end of *The Waste Land,* control, in both the sense of self-control and in the control of others.

9. Michael S. Reynolds, *The Sun Also Rises* (Boston: Twayne, 1988), pp. 26–31, 94.

Chapter 3: To the Pinnacle of Success and Beyond

1. Anthology readers must realize that stories printed are chosen for a number of reasons, including, but not limited to, the personal preferences of the editor(s). Equally important, the willingness of an author to be represented, or of his or her publisher to release a story at a reasonable fee, determines the selection. Some anthology publishers have included unrepresentative stories simply because they have had access to the copyright, or because a particular story was in the public domain. Choice of "The Killers," however, was largely justified.

2. Manuel Garcia was the real name of the bullfighter Maera, whom Hemingway had seen and admired, and who appears in *In Our Time,* chapters 13 and 14, dying of a goring in the latter, although the real Maera died of tuberculosis. Hemingway also includes him in *Death in the Afternoon.*

3. "An Essay in Criticism," The New York *Herald* (October 9, 1927), Book Section, pp. 1, 8.

4. Robert Frost, "The Figure a Poem Makes," *Complete Poems of Robert Frost* (New York: Holt, Rinehart and Winston, 1949), p. vi. Frost, too, speaks of ecstasy.

5. Philosopher William Barrett includes "A Clean Well-Lighted Place" in his study of existentialism, *Irrational Man* (Garden City: Doubleday-Anchor, 1958), pp. 55 and 251; he mentions *A Farewell to Arms,* too, p. 39.

6. Carlos Baker, *Ernest Hemingway: A Life Story* (New York: Scribner's, 1969), p. 352.

Chapter 4: Depressing Times

1. Philip Young, *Ernest Hemingway: A Reconsideration* (New York: Harcourt, Brace, 1952, 1966), p. 100.
2. George Plimpton, ed. *Writers at Work: The "Paris Review" Interviews*, 2nd series (New York: Viking, 1963), p. 239.
3. Scribner's, Hemingway's lifelong publisher, no longer issues this volume. The play is now published in a volume called *The Fifth Column and Four Stories of the Spanish Civil War* (New York: Scribner's, 1969), together with four stories written at the same time as the play but not published with it in the original short story collection. The page numbers of the following quotations come from this modern edition.
4. Scribner's published a volume of these stories called *The Snows of Kilimanjaro and Other Stories*, containing these African stories, in 1961.
5. The multiplication of names for those involved demands some explanation, and some historical background would probably be helpful as well. Spain was nominally a monarchy, ruled in name by Alfonso XIII, but actually governed by his prime minister, the dictator Primo de Rivera, who ruled Spain from 1923–30. The worldwide economic depression and the loss of army support caused Primo de Rivera's loss of power and, following a brief period of caretaker government, the abdication of Alfonso as well. An elected government refashioned Spain as a Republic in 1931, but was unable to contain clashing factions of conservative church, landowners, and military on the one hand, and peasants, workers, socialists, communists, and anarchists on the other. There were revolts against the government in the mining areas of Asturias along the Atlantic coast on the north and in the Catalan region of Barcelona along the Mediterranean coast on the east, and these revolts were suppressed by the military, including a young general from Spain's African colony of Morocco, Francisco Franco. A new Republic was formed in 1936, but it, too, could not contain the various factions, strikes, and outbursts of violence. In July 1936, the army generals announced a military takeover, and had it succeeded, there would have been no civil war, but the workers and peasants had had a

taste of government, and in the center and east of the country, successfully withstood the military. So, the Republicans were the political left, the Loyalists, allied with socialists and communists. The Nationalists were the Rebels, the political right, Fascists, and Falangists. Both Communists and Fascists outside Spain supported their sides, sending advisers and war matériel, Mussolini even sending Italian troops. The Fascists were much more successful in bringing in arms to help their side than were the Communists and ultimately won the war.

Chapter 5: Up to the End

1. Ernest Hemingway, *Men at War* (New York: Bramhall House, 1955), p. xi. Subsequent quotations will be paginated in the text and will refer to this edition.
2. Young, *Hemingway: A Reconsideration,* p. 114.
3. Baker, *Ernest Hemingway: A Life Story,* p. 500.
4. "The Christmas Gift," *Look* (18:8) April 20, 1954: pp. 29–37; (18:9) May 4, 1954: pp. 79–89.
5. *Atlantic,* vol. 200, November 1957.
6. The word counts vary from source to source. Carlos Baker in *Life Story* says the original manuscript was 120,000 words, the edited one 70,000 (pp. 552–53). Michener, in his introduction to the 1985 *The Dangerous Summer* has 120,000 and 70,000 (p. 13). Hotchner, who did the editing, says the manuscript was 108,746 words, 688 typed pages, which was cut to 53,830 words for the editors of *Life* to make their final excisions (Hotchner, *Papa Hemingway* [New York: Random House, 1966], pp. 239–42).

Chapter 6: The Posthumous Works

1. Jacqueline Tavernier-Courbin, "The Manuscripts of *A Moveable Feast,*" *Hemingway notes* 6 (Spring, 1981): pp. 9–15; and "Fact and Fiction in *A Moveable Feast,*" *The Hemingway Review* 4 (Fall, 1984): pp. 44–51. Gerry Brenner, "Are We Going to Hemingway's *Feast?*" *American Literature* 54 (December 1982): pp. 528–44.
2. Mary Welsh Hemingway, *How It Was* (New York: Ballantine Books, 1977), p. 659.
3. Tavernier-Courbin, *Hemingway Review,* p. 46.

4. Ernest Hemingway, *A Moveable Feast* (New York: Scribners, 1964), p. ix.

5. Brenner, "Are We Going to Hemingway's *Feast?*" p. 531.

6. One, in fact, has been plainly disproved. Hemingway writes of the bartender of the Ritz Hotel bar asking Hemingway who is this Fitzgerald that people ask him about, for he doesn't remember Fitzgerald. This is clearly not true since others, including a French PhD student at the Sorbonne, interviewed the bartender, who clearly remembered Fitzgerald (cited by Tavernier-Courbin, *Hemingway Review* [fall 1984, 50, note 25]). This fictional construction of Hemingway underscores to his own lasting fame, superior to Fitzgerald's.

7. For a full bibliographic citation to each, please consult the bibliography.

8. Ernest Hemingway, *Islands in the Stream* (New York: Scribner's, 1970), editor's introductory, unpaged note. Two sections of the novel were published in magazines, one prior to book publication: in *Esquire*, October 1970, an abridgement of "Bimini," and in *Cosmopolitan*, March 1971, a condensation of "Cuba."

9. Carlos Baker in *Hemingway: The Writer as Artist* 4th ed., (Princeton University Press, Princeton, NJ: 1972), p. 392, finds another parallel to *The Old Man and the Sea* in a remark of David's after his fish escapes. " 'Don't make yourself some sort of special guilt about it,' he tells his father. 'I just went too far out' " p. 96. But page 96 in *Islands* occurs before the fishing incident, and after Davy loses the fish I can find no such sentence in the published text.

10. Baker, *Life Story*, p. 364.

11. Ernest Hemingway, *The Dangerous Summer*, introduction James A. Michener (New York: Scribner's, 1985), p. 14. Subsequent quotations will refer to this edition and will be paginated in my text. The editor who cut the book text for Scribner's is Michael Pietsch.

12. All of these examples occur on p. 85 of the September 5, 1960, *Life* magazine and pp. 46 and 47 of the book.

13. Barbara Probst Solomon, "Where's Papa," *The New Republic* (March 9, 1987): pp. 30–34; the suggestion occurs on p. 32. This was a review of *The Garden of Eden*, and *The New Republic* put on its issue cover a picture of the dust jacket of *Garden* under the headline "The Great Hemingway Hoax." Echoing Michener on the unedited manuscript of *The Dan-*

gerous Summer, Solomon wrote, "There is no way that the manuscript I read, an extraordinary mass of unfinished work, . . . could have been made into a smooth popular novel" (p. 31).

Select Bibliography

Primary Sources

Three Stories and Ten Poems. Paris: Contact Publishing, 1923.
in our time. Paris: Three Mountains Press, 1924.
In Our Time. New York: Boni and Liveright, 1925.
The Torrents of Spring. New York: Scribner's, 1926.
The Sun Also Rises. New York: Scribner's, 1926.
Men Without Women. New York: Scribner's, 1927.
A Farewell to Arms. New York: Scribner's, 1929.
Death in the Afternoon. New York: Scribner's, 1932.
Winner Take Nothing. New York: Scribner's, 1933.
The Green Hills of Africa. New York: Scribner's, 1935.
To Have and Have Not. New York: Scribner's, 1937.
The Fifth Column and the First Forty-Nine Stories. New York: Scribner's, 1938.
For Whom the Bell Tolls. New York: Scribner's 1940.
Men at War. New York: Crown Publishers, 1942.
Across the River and into the Trees. New York: Scribner's, 1950.
The Old Man and the Sea. New York: Scribner's, 1952.
The Wild Years, ed. Gene Z. Hanrahan. New York: Dell, 1962.
A Moveable Feast. New York: Scribner's, 1964.
By-Line: Ernest Hemingway, ed. William White. New York: Scribner's, 1967.
Islands in the Stream. New York: Scribner's, 1970.
Ernest Hemingway, Cub Reporter, ed. Matthew J. Bruccoli. Pittsburgh: University of Pittsburgh Press, 1970.
Ernest Hemingway's Apprenticeship: Oak Park, 1916–1917, ed. Matthew J. Bruccoli. Washington: NCR, 1971.
The Nick Adams Stories, ed. Philip Young. New York: Scribner's, 1972.
Ernest Hemingway / Complete Poems, ed. Nicholas Gerogiannis. New York: Harcourt Brace Jovanovich, 1979.

Ernest Hemingway: Selected Letters, ed. Carlos Baker. New York: Scribner's, 1981.

Dateline: Toronto, ed. William White. New York: Scribner's, 1985.

The Dangerous Summer. New York: Scribner's, 1985.

The Garden of Eden. New York: Scribner's, 1986.

The Complete Short Stories of Ernest Hemingway, ed. Finca Vigía. New York: Scribner's, 1987.

Biographies

Baker, Carlos. *Ernest Hemingway: A Life Story.* New York: Scribner's, 1969.

Reynolds, Michael. *The Young Hemingway.* London: Basil Blackwell, 1986. The first volume to be printed of three.

Criticism

Baker, Carlos. *Hemingway: The Writer as Artist.* 4th ed. Princeton: Princeton University Press, 1972.

Young, Philip. *Ernest Hemingway: A Reconsideration.* New York: Harcourt, Brace & World, 1966.

Rovit, Earl & Brenner, Gerry. *Ernest Hemingway.* Boston: Twayne, 1986.

Index